9. 8-5 8

WORSHIP SERVICES
FOR
JUNIOR HIGHS

WORSHIP SERVICES
FOR
JUNIOR HIGHS

By
Alice Anderson Bays

ABINGDON PRESS
NEW YORK • NASHVILLE

WORSHIP SERVICES FOR JUNIOR HIGHS

Copyright © MCMLVIII by Abingdon Press

Library of Congress Catalog Card Number: 58-10454

SET UP, PRINTED, AND BOUND BY THE
PARTHENON PRESS, AT NASHVILLE,
TENNESSEE, UNITED STATES OF AMERICA

To
My Grandsons
ROBERT AND GEOFFREY BAYS

PREFACE

This is the eighth volume in a series of worship services for youth. It is the aim of the author that junior highs may be led to a growing conception of God, find greater meaning in worship, and take their place in the building of the kingdom of God on earth.

These services are prepared for use in the church school, in evening sessions of youth groups, and in summer camps. They may be adapted to local situations and used to supplement worship suggestions of denominational boards. They may be shortened by omitting certain parts or used as an anthology by lifting out a poem, story, or other selection. The prayers may be used as suggestions from which youth may form their own prayers.

This book has grown out of actual experiences with teen-agers in local churches and other places of worship. It may be used in small as well as in larger churches. The worship services in this book are grouped into three series, the aims of which are: Series One—to guide junior highs to a better understanding of the way God works through persons; Series Two—to lead youth to a conception of God at work in the world and to find their part in building the kingdom of God on earth; Series Three—to help youth think of holidays as days set apart to be observed with religious connotation. It is hoped that through the use of these services God will become real to youth through finding their part in bringing his kingdom to their own community.

I wish to acknowledge indebtedness and to express gratitude to all who have assisted in the preparation of this volume—to the youth of First Methodist Church, Oak Ridge, Tennessee; to my son, Robert, for literary criticism; to Elizabeth Jones Oakberg for reading the manuscript and for valuable suggestions. Grateful acknowledgment is made to authors and publishers who have been generous in granting permission to use copyrighted material. Every effort has been made to trace ownership of all material and to give proper credit.

ALICE ANDERSON BAYS

Oak Ridge, Tennessee

SUGGESTIONS FOR COUNSELOR

A leader or counselor has an opportunity to direct the growth of boys and girls as they learn about God and find ways of expressing themselves in worship. Discovery of God is an individual matter in which a leader may help, but everyone must find his own path to God. The adult may share, but each person makes his own contact with the Deity.

Worship is not something that a leader may perform for another. It is a two-way proposition in which God speaks and each person makes his own response. Worship is the hungry heart reaching out to contact God. Within people there is a desire to worship something beyond themselves—something greater and wiser than themselves. Augustine said, "Thou, O God, hast made us for thyself and we are restless until we find thee."

Certain criteria are important as a yardstick in order to improve group worship. Can we answer these questions in the affirmative?

Do we feel our need of God?

Can we get rid of distracting thoughts and turn our minds toward God?

Do we receive help in solving problems?

Have we discovered God's will and purpose for our lives?

Do we approach God in an expectant attitude?

Are we growing in Christlike character?

The following questions might be criteria for a leader of worship:

Have I a spirit of worship as I strive to lead others?

Does God have a definite place in my life, and do I spend sufficient time in communion with him?

What is my goal as I attempt to lead others in worship?

What growth and development may I expect in the persons of my group?

There is a wide variation in training, experience, and awareness of God among the teen-agers in our groups. Some are able already to lead, but there are others who have had little experience. Those with limited training may help to prepare the room for worship, build worship centers, and help in planning worship. Through doing these tasks they will grow in skill and eventually be able to lead.

Tasks may be assigned to timid persons that will give them satisfying experiences, and gradually they will be able to take more difficult projects. A fear of failure causes some to refuse to take any part. A leader or counselor would not ask anyone to have a part in worship to show off his talent. It is well to avoid elaborate introductions in worship. Instead of centering attention on persons taking part, the aim is to lead the group into an awareness of the presence of God.

How should prayer be used? Are teen-agers being trained in the proper use of prayer? For what should they pray? In prayer we should not attempt to bend God to our wills, but rather strive to find his will for our lives. The highest use of prayer is to bring ourselves to the place where we are willing to live by the will and purpose of God.

How may we help junior highs to establish a habit of Bible reading? From our attitude toward the Bible they may learn to find value in reading the Scriptures. Can we not also help them to discover various types of literature, its rich store of knowledge, and interesting stories in the Bible? We may need to give some of them experiences in finding passages so they can learn how to use the Bible.

Scriptures should be carefully selected for worship with the needs of the group in mind. The age and understanding of the group should be considered also. Modern translations may be used if they make the meaning clearer to the group. Some passages may be spoken in unison while others lend themselves to choral reading.

Worship may be improved greatly by using care in the selection of hymns. The music should be within the range of the voices of the group, and it should be tuneful and of good quality. The words of the hymn should carry forward the message of the service. Many suitable hymns are made available through a study of the hymnal and learning new hymns occasionally.

The call to worship should call the attention of the group away from themselves and direct it toward God. It may be a suitable passage of scripture, a poem, or a prose selection that suggests worship and is related to the theme.

The poetry selected should not be too difficult for teen-agers to understand, and it should express ideas within the range of their experience. The poems should challenge or stimulate the thinking of the group.

Simplicity should be the keynote of the worship center, and it should relate to the theme of the service. Too many objects tend to clutter up the center and defeat the purpose, which is to help the group concentrate on the subject or theme. If the service is held at night, a strong light focused upon the center will help to hold the attention of the group.

Distractions should be kept at a minimum if possible. Latecomers should be seated in the back, and those who assist in the service should be seated in the front. There should be no jarring bells at the beginning or at the close of the service.

The leader of worship may ask himself the following questions as criteria in preparation for a service:

Is the room in order and properly ventilated?

Have I kept in mind the needs of the group?

Have I selected the best material that is available?

Are all details provided for ahead of time?

Have I taken into account the amount of time available?

Is my aim or purpose for this service worthy?

Has my plan been approved by the worship committee?

Have I planned for a high point of emphasis in the service?

Am I sincere and does my life conform to the message of the service?

Junior high youth should assume as much leadership in worship as their training and skill will permit. With coaching from the counselor several members of the group will develop skill and be able to tell stories acceptably. They should begin studying in time so as to absorb the message of the story. Instead of memorizing the story the message should be presented in the words of the storyteller. With practice teen-agers learn to forget themselves and center their attention upon the message they hope to convey.

What results may we expect in the lives of junior high youth as they worship together? Should there not be a change in their attitudes and actions as they find God and commune regularly with him? They have reached the age when they can be helped to choose the direction of their lives. They are able to choose to follow the will of God or their own wills. When they decide to let God's spirit dominate their lives, follow the example and teaching of Christ, they are ready to make a public commitment and join the church.

When teen-agers make this decision, spiritual values take on greater significance, new insights are acquired, and strength is gained to meet daily problems. The decision to let God rule in their lives helps to replace bad habits with Christian ways of living.

Leaders of worship have the high privilege of working with God and co-operating with parents and teachers in the interpretation of God's plan of salvation to junior high youth.

CONTENTS

13

AROUND THE YEAR WITH GOD

GOD SPEAKS TO US

SERVICE 1

GOD SPEAKS
THROUGH A SCIENTIST

PRELUDE: "Berceuse" (Iljinsky)

CALL TO WORSHIP:
> He that dwelleth in the secret place of the most High
> shall abide under the shadow of the Almighty.
> I will say of the Lord, He is my refuge and my fortress:
> my God; in him will I trust.[1]

HYMN: "Holy Spirit, Truth Divine" or
"Now in the Days of Youth"

SCRIPTURE:
Bless the Lord, O my soul. O Lord my God, thou art very great;
thou art clothed with honour and majesty.

Who coverest thyself with light as with a garment: who stretchest
out the heavens like a curtain: . . .

Who laid the foundations of the earth, that it should not be
removed for ever. . . .

He watereth the hills from his chambers: the earth is satisfied with
the fruit of thy works.

He causeth the grass to grow for the cattle, and herb for the
service of man: that he may bring forth food out of the earth. . . .

O Lord, how manifold are thy works! in wisdom hast thou made
them all: the earth is full of thy riches. . . .

I will sing unto the Lord as long as I live: I will sing praise to
my God while I have my being.[2]

17

POEM:

Who knows the deepest secrets that reside in every heart?
Who knows what cares beset us, though we live our lives apart?
Who knows—before we voice them—our every wish and whim?
God knows, and gives us guidance when we give our hearts to
him.

Who speaks throughout the ages in accents clear and still?
Who speaks to every human heart that surrenders its self-will?
Who speaks to each condition with insight wise and rare?
God speaks; let us listen as we turn to him in prayer.[3]

—ROBERT A. KNOWLES

LEADER:

We will hear the story of a scientist who searched for truth throughout his lifetime. Let us notice how God spoke to him and revealed
secrets that were unknown before. If we develop our talents and
live close to God, is it not possible that we might also be a channel
through which God would reveal truths to the world?

STORY:

GEORGE WASHINGTON CARVER, A SCIENTIST

George Washington Carver, the son of a slave, was born on the
Diamond Grove Plantation in Missouri. He and his mother were
stolen by slave raiders from their owner, Moses Carver. The mother
was never heard of again, but he was returned to his owner in exchange for a horse. He lived with the Carvers, helped with the
chores and worked in his little garden, until ten years of age, when
he went to nearby Neosho to go to school.

The boy was so hungry to learn that he soon mastered his first
book, a speller. In two years he had learned all he could from his
teacher. Going to Fort Scott, Kansas, he supported himself by cook-
ing and laundering until he finished high school. Applying for
admission to a college in Iowa, he was turned down because he
was a Negro.

At Simpson College, Indianola, Iowa, George was accepted, and
after paying his modest fee, he had ten cents left. For a week he
lived on corn meal and beef suet, which he bought with his last dime.
He lived in a woodshed near the campus, but later moved to a loft
over a livery stable. A woman loaned him a washtub and board with
which he earned his expenses by doing laundry for the students.

After graduation from Simpson College he went to Iowa State College, where he received his Master's degree in science. Here he was given a teaching position and was the first Negro to serve on the faculty. Although this college offered him everything he had dreamed of, he left to go to Tuskegee to work with his own race.

Upon arrival at Tuskegee, Carver saw enough to challenge anyone who wanted to serve. Everywhere there was evidence of poverty. There were a few buildings but no equipment. Patiently he began to build a department of scientific agriculture. His pupils brought in bottles and wire salvaged from rubbish heaps, and from these Carver made their equipment for the laboratory.

Carver began to show the pupils how to make the most out of what they had. He taught them to make fertilizer from swampy muck, paint from native clay, paper from tomato vines, marble from shavings, and many other useful things from cast-off material. He inspired young teachers to go out and teach the poor farmers of the South how to rotate crops, build up the soil, and provide a balanced diet for their families.

Later Carver taught less and less and gave more time to his experiments. From the peanut, the poor man's food that grew in abundance in Alabama, he produced more than three hundred useful products. Among them were milk, ice cream, coffee, face powder, printer's ink, dyes, soap, wood stains, and so on. He also extracted an oil that helped to restore usefulness to limbs that had been crippled by polio. From the sweet potato over one hundred useful products came, among them four kinds of flour, three kinds of breakfast foods, molasses, chocolate, and rubber.

Carver showed the Negroes how to supplement their diet with wild herbs that grew near their homes. All of his discoveries were made available without cost. When peanut growers sent him large checks for service rendered, he returned them promptly, saying, "All that I know has come from God, and I cannot take anything for it."

Edison offered Carver a position at a fabulous salary and urged him to come to his East Orange laboratory, saying, "Come with me, and together we will unlock the secrets of the universe." It may have been difficult for the young scientist to turn down this offer, but he replied, saying, "My life is dedicated to the South, and my job here at Tuskegee is not finished." He remained the rest of his life at a salary of about three thousand dollars a year, for money did not mean much to him. Out of his meager salary he saved thirty thousand dollars, which he left to Tuskegee.

John O. Gross mentions four things that Dr. Carver took to college—things that money cannot buy, but which are essential for a successful college experience:

He brought to college an *inquiring mind,* an eagerness to learn. He was interested in finding out all he could about many things. It is amazing what he was able to learn in a lifetime. He was an accomplished musician, an artist, a teacher, and a scientist.

Young Carver took to college a *desire to help himself.* Throughout his life he was self-reliant. His washtub experience at college showed that he preferred to make his own way. When gifts were offered him, he refused them, for all he wanted was a chance to earn his own expenses.

The young man also took to college a *willingness to accept guidance.* He enjoyed painting and had skill, for some of his paintings hang in famous museums in Europe. However, when one of his teachers convinced him that he could serve better in the field of agriculture, he locked up his paints and brushes and did not go near them for an entire year. This decision was not easy to make.

Carver brought to college a *desire to serve,* to help his race get rid of poverty, to develop its talents, and to use its meager resources to the best advantage. This is the reason that he turned down Edison's offer and stayed at Tuskegee.

When he was asked, "What happened in the beginning at Simpson College to help you?" Carver replied, "Simpson College helped me to realize that I was a human being." And that was a great gift for a college to make. In spite of a frail body and with little encouragement he developed many skills and overcame more difficulties than most people have to face.

A visitor at Tuskegee inquired of Carver, "How have you been able to discover so many secrets that were unknown before?" He replied, "I am God's interpreter, an instrument in his hands. When I go to my laboratory, I do not need to take textbooks. I ask God to reveal to me the necessary steps to take, to guide me in my research, and he shows me what to do. What I am doing here is through him who gave me a vision fifty years ago while I was attending Simpson College. I begin each day in communion with God, listening to his direction, and following his suggestions. If I can I take a walk, and it is at that time that I receive guidance for the day."

Carver's willingness to accept guidance from God has made his life one of great usefulness and helped him to become one of the outstanding scientists of his country. He believed that God would help him find a way of helping others. He had genius and greatness of spirit which made him a useful worker in God's kingdom.[4]

POEM:

> God, the Lord of lowly places,
> Speak to us through common things,
> Thou through whom a manger cradle
> Joined the shepherds with the kings.
> Make us humble; make us faithful;
> Guide to all man's journeyings.
>
> God, the Lord of prayerful living,
> Gird us for the task begun,
> As of old on Olive's mountain
> Thou didst strengthen Christ thy Son.
> Make us humble, make us faithful;
> Striving that thy will be done.[5]
>
> —JANET THURBER

PRAYER:

Our Father, we thank thee for a scientist like Carver, who gave his life in service of others. We are grateful that he was not content with a life of ease when members of his race were in need. Help us to feel the burden of poverty and find ways of doing our part. When we think of how much thou hast done for us and the many people who need help, lead us in ways of sharing our time and energy to help the poor. May we be willing to accept guidance from thee and be an instrument in thy hands to help where the need is great. Grant us strength and courage to heed thy call for Christian service; through Jesus we pray. AMEN.

HYMN: "O Jesus, I Have Promised" or
"Just as I Am, Thine Own to Be"

BENEDICTION:

Dismiss us with thy blessing and may thy will and purpose be done in our lives. AMEN.

SERVICE 2

GOD SPEAKS THROUGH MUSIC

PRELUDE: "Larghetto" from Sonata in D (Handel)

CALL TO WORSHIP:

> O come, let us sing unto the Lord:
> Let us make a joyful noise to the rock of our salvation.
> Let us come before his presence with thanksgiving, and
> make a joyful noise unto him with psalms. . . .
> O come, let us worship and bow down:
> Let us kneel before the Lord our maker.[1]

POEM:

> Jesus, we look to thee,
>   Thy promised presence claim;
> Thou in the midst of us shalt be,
>   Assembled in thy name.
>
> . . . .
>
> Present we know thou art;
>   But, O, thyself reveal!
> Now, Lord, let ev'ry waiting heart
>   The mighty comfort feel.
> —CHARLES WESLEY

HYMN: "O for a Thousand Tongues to Sing" or
"Christ, Whose Glory Fills the Skies"

SCRIPTURE:

O sing unto the Lord a new song: sing unto the Lord, all the earth.
Sing unto the Lord, bless his name; shew forth his salvation from day to day.

Declare his glory among the heathen, his wonders among all people.

For the Lord is great, and greatly to be praised: he is to be feared above all gods.

For all the gods of the nations are idols: but the Lord made the heavens.

Honour and majesty are before him: strength and beauty are in his sanctuary.

Give unto the Lord, O ye kindreds of the people, give unto the Lord glory and strength.

Give unto the Lord the glory due unto his name: bring an offering, and come into his courts.

O worship the Lord in the beauty of holiness: fear before him, all the earth.[2]

LEADER:

Henry Ward Beecher said, "I would rather have written 'Jesus, Lover of My Soul' than to have all the fame of all the kings that ever lived." We will hear the story of the writer of this hymn, "God's Troubadour," the song writer of Methodism.

STORY:

GOD'S TROUBADOUR

Charles Wesley was born at Epworth, England, about 250 years ago, the eighteenth child of Samuel and Susannah Wesley. Growing up in a literary family helped prepare him to be the song writer of Methodism. His brothers and sisters wrote to one another in verse, and he thought in rhyme and meter. There was a poetic strain running through the entire family.

At nine years of age the lad was sent to Westminster School in London, where his brother Samuel was teaching. When he and his brother John later graduated from Oxford, both became ministers. They came to America to work with General James Oglethorpe in his colony in Georgia.

The young man wrote his first poem at Oxford, and for the next forty years there was scarcely a day that he did not write one. Much of the power of the early Methodists came from the hymns he wrote. The people who had droned out the psalms were glad to sing his songs, set to joyous tunes and with words they could understand. The Methodists sang a new day into Britain.

Large crowds came to hear Charles preach, and his hymns found a ready response with the people. The uneducated masses could understand the beliefs of Methodism and express their religious feelings through singing his hymns.

Charles and John were converted about the same time. At once Charles wrote a hymn about his experience. Later John rushed in to tell of his conversion, and together they sang the song that Charles had just written. This is called the birth song of Methodism and is still popular in England. Another song on the same subject and popular with us today is "O for a Thousand Tongues to Sing."

Charles was able to write hymns on practically any subject. There were many ideas about "Christian perfection." As was his custom, Charles wrote a song to make this idea clear and easy to understand. The following hymn was written with this purpose in mind:

> O for a heart to praise my God,
>   A heart from sin set free,
> A heart that always feels thy blood
>   So freely shed for me!
>
> .   .   .   .
>
> A heart in every thought renewed,
>   And full of love divine;
> Perfect, and right, and pure, and good,
>   A copy, Lord, of thine!
>
> Thy nature, gracious Lord, impart;
>   Come quickly from above,
> Write thy new Name upon my heart,
>   Thy new, best Name of Love.

This song writer wrote some of his hymns to fit the joyous folk tunes that the people already knew. He said, "Why should the devil have all of the good tunes?" There were a warmth and enthusiasm in the Methodist meetings because the people sang instead of having a choir sing for them. The hymns were happy expressions of inward experiences.

Wesley often came hurriedly on horseback to the Methodist headquarters at City Road in London and called for pen and ink. He had composed a hymn while in the saddle and wanted to write it down while it was still on his mind. Many of his hymns are sung by all faiths and are greatly loved today. "Christ the Lord Is Risen Today" and "Hark! the Herald Angels Sing" are favorites and found in most hymnals. The following is sung by many groups today:

GOD SPEAKS THROUGH MUSIC

Ye servants of God, your Master proclaim,
And publish abroad his wonderful Name;
The Name all-victorious of Jesus extol;
His kingdom is glorious, and rules over all.

. . . .

Then let us adore, and give him his right,
All glory and power, all wisdom and might,
All honor and blessing, with angels above,
And thanks never ceasing for infinite love.

This prolific hymn writer published fifty hymnals and wrote over six thousand hymns. *The Methodist Hymnal* in America contains fifty-six of his hymns. The following is popular with youth today:

A charge to keep I have,
  A God to glorify,
A never-dying soul to save,
  And fit it for the sky.

To serve the present age,
  My calling to fulfill;
O may it all my powers engage
  To do my Master's will!

. . . .

Help me to watch and pray,
  And on thyself rely,
Assured, if I my trust betray,
  I shall forever die.

This man who walked with God is considered one of the greatest hymn writers of all times. He preached and wrote to the close of his life. The last thing that he did at the end of a long and useful life was to dictate a hymn to his wife. He has encouraged and inspired many people by the hymns he wrote.

LEADER:
We will sing a new hymn written by James Boeringer of the Lutheran Church to the tune of the hymn "Saviour, Again to Thy Dear Name We Raise." This hymn was written for use during National Youth Week.

Hymn:

> O Father, Son, and Holy Spirit, hear;
>   Thou who dost know our doubting and our grief,
> Grant the petition of each heart sincere:
>   "Lord, I believe; help thou mine unbelief."
>
> Should faith in Christ's redemption fall away;
>   And fear devour, and doubt come like a thief
> To steal our peace and joy, help each to pray:
>   "Lord, I believe; help thou mine unbelief."
>
> Our Father, from pride's bondage set us free,
>   Since any man of sinners might be chief;
> Humble our souls that each may cry to thee:
>   "Lord, I believe; help thou mine unbelief."
>
> Dear Son of God, who in Gethsemane
>   Didst bear our burdens, finding no relief;
> Destroy temptation's pow'r and hear each plea:
>   "Lord, I believe; help thou mine unbelief."
>
> O Holy Spirit, grace bestow that we
>   May grow in faith, though years of life be brief—
> Till faith shall lead to sight, our prayer shall be:
>   "Lord, I believe; help thou mine unbelief." [3]
>   —James Boeringer

Poem:

> Life is a song that we sing;
> Each passing day the staff upon which the notes
>   of daily thoughts and deeds are laid;
> And passing by, in the hurrying throng
> Are the fellow men upon whose hearts each song is
>   played,
> With dissonant beat—or melody sweet,
> As conflicts come—or heart with heart doth meet.
>
> O sing a new song unto the Lord;
> Be not still!
> Lift your life in joyful praise,
> Fraught with promise of a better life,

In accord with God's own will.
Sing a new song;
Let your life blend
In harmony with God's great purpose for life that
has no end.[4]

—ROBERT A. KNOWLES

PRAYER:

Our Father, we thank thee for the great musicians who have dedicated their talent to thee. We thank thee for men like Charles Wesley who have helped people to know thee through hymns. Speak to us and help us better to understand thee through singing the great hymns of the church. Help us to take the message of these servants of thine and practice it in daily living. May we like them use our talents and skill to bring others close to thee. Take our lips and speak to those who have never known thee; take our minds and think through them; take our hearts and love thy needy children through them. Help us in our study, work, and play to keep thy purpose before us. In Jesus' name we pray. AMEN.

HYMN: "Love Divine, All Loves Excelling" or
"O for a Heart to Praise My God"

BENEDICTION:

Dismiss us with thy blessing; fill our hearts with joy and may our lips sing thy praise. AMEN.

SERVICE 3

GOD SPEAKS THROUGH SERVICE

PRELUDE: Hymn tune "St. Theodulph"

CALL TO WORSHIP:

> Draw thou my soul, O Christ,
> Closer to thine;
> Breathe into every wish
> Thy will divine!
> Raise my low self above,
> Won by thy deathless love;
> Ever, O Christ, through mine
> Let thy life shine.
>
> Lead forth my soul, O Christ,
> One with thine own,
> Joyful to follow thee
> Through paths unknown!
> In thee my strength renew;
> Give me my work to do!
> Through me thy truth be shown,
> Thy love made known.
>   —LUCY LARCOM

HYMN: "Break Thou the Bread of Life" or
       "Work, for the Night Is Coming"

INVOCATION:
  Our Father, we thank thee for this time of worship. Speak to each of us and reveal thy will to us. Make us eager to receive and carry

28

out the ideas coming from thee. Help us to know thee through thy Word, through the talks and stories we hear, through the hymns we sing, and through the lives of others. Speak to us in this worship service. In Jesus' name, we pray. AMEN.

SCRIPTURE:

I beseech you therefore, brethren, by the mercies of God, that ye present your bodies a living sacrifice, holy, acceptable unto God, which is your reasonable service.

And be not conformed to this world: but be ye transformed by the renewing of your mind, that ye may prove what is that good, and acceptable, and perfect will of God. . . .

Whosoever will be great among you, let him be your minister.

And whosoever will be chief among you, let him be your servant: even as the Son of man came not to be ministered unto, but to minister, and to give his life a ransom for many. . . .

No man can serve two masters: for either he will hate the one, and love the other; or else he will hold to the one, and despise the other. Ye cannot serve God and mammon.[1]

LEADER:

A generation ago there were many boys and girls in the hill section of the South who were not in school. Martha Berry saw this need and did something about it.

STORY:

MARTHA BERRY OPENED DOORS TO BOYS AND GIRLS

Martha Berry, the daughter of a well-to-do planter in Rome, Georgia, was expected to live in ease and comfort. But she could not sit idly by when she saw the children of the nearby country growing up in poverty and ignorance. Because no one else felt the need of helping them, she took the task upon herself.

One Sunday afternoon while playing the melodeon in her log-cabin playhouse, she saw poorly clad mountain children outside the window listening. Inviting them in, she played for them and told them stories from the Bible. On the following Sunday they were back for more, and when the number grew, she moved to a church at Possum Trot. Seeing that the children needed more than Bible stories, she built a school for them across the highway on land that her father had given to her.

The Berry School began in a one-room cabin that the older pupils built from lumber cut from the land. Miss Berry noticed that many of the children were kept at home to help on the farm and others were absent during the winter months when the roads were bad. In 1902 a boarding school was built where the children could live throughout the year.

To many of her friends Miss Berry seemed unprepared for the task she had assumed. Having lived a sheltered life she had never done hard physical labor, and she had no previous business training. But she took upon herself the total burden of the school and developed the necessary skill as the enrollment grew and the work increased.

Against the advice of her lawyer Martha Berry deeded her land to the school. When the lawyer argued, she remarked, "I shall raise a better crop than the land is producing now." The school had to be self-sustaining because the pupils came from homes of low incomes, so she set about to raise the money needed.

In the beginning the tuition was only twenty-five dollars a year, which was more than most of the pupils could pay. Some brought a pig, a team of oxen, or a load of corn, and worked to pay the remainder. In this way they were taught "not to be ministered unto, but to minister."

As the school grew, Miss Berry spent more time raising money for additional buildings. In New York City she talked to a Wall Street man who gave her five hundred dollars and the names of others who would help. After she had told her story to Theodore Roosevelt, he gave a dinner for her in the White House. She made an appeal for help, and the men at the table wrote checks for large sums of money. On one occasion Andrew Carnegie offered her fifty thousand dollars for the school, provided she would raise a like amount. She told her story to Mrs. Russell Sage, who gave one half of the sum, and the remainder was raised in a short while.

Returning from a Florida vacation, Henry Ford and his wife visited the Berry School. Following a delicious meal Mrs. Ford took her husband to the kitchen, where she showed him the old range. She remarked, "Henry, think of all that wonderful food cooked on this old stove. They need a new one."

"Well," he replied, "why don't you give them one?"

A few weeks later Miss Berry received a letter from Mrs. Ford asking what building was needed. Miss Berry replied, "A dormitory is needed, but perhaps I am putting the cart before the horse, since a new kitchen is needed as well." Another letter came saying that the Fords would give a new kitchen and a dormitory. A few years later other buildings were added until there was a total of five buildings, which made up the Quadrangle. They include two dormitories, a dining hall, a kitchen, classrooms, and a recreational building.

In addition to the original one hundred acres that her father gave to her, Miss Berry bought thirty thousand acres that she planted in orchards and pine trees. More than one hundred buildings erected by the students stand on the campus, which is one of the most beautiful in the South.

The growth of this school from a one-room log cabin to a high school and college is a miracle. It has a program of self-help, for the students do all the work and learn while studying four days a week and working two. The girls cook, sew, spin, weave, operate the school laundry, work as secretaries, and conduct a nursery for faculty members. In this way the pupils gain useful knowledge and learn profitable trades.

Under the direction of certain teachers the boys cut the trees, haul them to the sawmill, and out of the lumber furniture or buildings are made. Boys learn to be masons while putting up buildings. Others operate the farm, which has one thousand acres in crops, two thousand acres in pasture, three hundred in fruit trees, and forty in vegetables.

Since Miss Berry's death in 1942 a balance has been kept between work and play under the wise leadership of the president. It is still a rule that only those who cannot afford to go to school elsewhere are accepted. From the beginning well-trained teachers, dedicated to the task, have been employed. There are 150 teachers and more than 1000 students.

Among the fifteen thousand graduates of the Berry School there are doctors, lawyers, judges, teachers, ministers, farmers, writers, secretaries, and members of other professions. Some have even gone into foreign fields of service, while others remain at the school to teach and serve in other capacities.

Miss Berry never allowed any other interest to interfere with her dream of making an education available to the boys and girls of the hill country. All that came from her father's estate and forty years of her life were spent in making this dream come true. The result of her effort and that of those who worked with her is that the lives of these pupils have been enriched. They have also been trained for a vocation, taught to be good citizens, and fitted to render useful service to their country.

The gate of opportunity is open wide at the Berry School to poor boys and girls who are willing to work while they learn. Thousands of friends everywhere keep this gate open, not only through the gifts of their means, but through the gift of themselves—their own warm interest. In Martha Berry's own words, her school has remained "rich in friends."

POEM:

> O God, who workest hitherto,
>   Working in all we see
> Fain would we be and bear and do,
>   As best it pleaseth thee.
>
> .   .   .   .
>
> Our skill of hand and strength of limb
>   Are not our own, but thine;
> We link them to the work of him
>   Who made all life divine!
>   —THOMAS W. FRECKLETON

LEADER:

We are grateful for the privilege of helping to keep open the doors of opportunity to boys and girls who otherwise would not get to go to college. Through our offering today we make it possible for other students to be admitted to the Berry School. As we think of these students, let us remember the words of Jesus when he said, "Lay not up for yourselves treasures upon earth, where moth and rust doth corrupt, and where thieves break through and steal: but lay up for yourselves treasures in heaven, where neither moth nor rust doth corrupt, and where thieves do not break through nor steal: for where your treasure is, there will your heart be also." [2]

OFFERING [3]

HYMN: "O Master, Let Me Walk with Thee" or
       "Lord, Speak to Me That I May Speak"

PRAYER:

Our Father, we are thankful for persons like Martha Berry who opened doors of opportunity to boys and girls who otherwise would have missed them. Bless and prosper the school to which she gave her life and her possessions. We thank thee for those who labored with her to bring the light of knowledge to young people held back by poverty. Bless and strengthen all who are working in Christian colleges. Open our eyes to the needs of this group and help us to be faithful in supporting Christian colleges. In the name of him who came not to be ministered unto, but to minister, we pray. AMEN.

BENEDICTION:

Now may the light that shone in Jesus Christ our Lord shine in our hearts and minds. AMEN.

SERVICE 4

GOD SPEAKS
THROUGH SELF-CONTROL

PRELUDE: Hymn tune "Hyfrydol"

CALL TO WORSHIP:

Remember now thy Creator in the days of thy youth, while the evil days come not, nor the years draw nigh, when thou shalt say, I have no pleasure in them . . . . Fear God, and keep his commandments: for this is the whole duty of man. For God shall bring every work into judgment, with every secret thing, whether it be good, or whether it be evil. . . .

Let no man despise thy youth; but be thou an example of the believers, in word, in conversation, in charity, in spirit, in faith, in purity. . . . Neglect not the gift that is in thee.[1]

HYMN: "The Voice of God Is Calling" or
"O Young and Fearless Prophet"

RESPONSIVE READING:

Leader: He that is slow to anger is better than the mighty; and he that ruleth his spirit than he that taketh a city. . . .

Group: Teach me to do thy will; . . . lead me into the land of uprightness. . . .

Leader: Keep thy heart with all diligence; for out of it are the issues of life. . . .

Group: Incline not my heart to any evil thing, to practise wicked works with men that work iniquity. . . .

Leader: Put away from thee a froward mouth, and perverse lips put far from thee. . . .

Group: Set a watch, O Lord, before my mouth; keep the door of my lips. . . .

Leader: My son, attend to my words; incline thine ear unto my sayings. . . . Keep them in the midst of thine heart. For they are life unto those that find them. . . .

Group: Teach me, O Lord, the way of thy statutes; and I shall keep it unto the end. Give me understanding, and I shall keep thy law; yea, I shall observe it with my whole heart.[2]

POEM:

Blest are the pure in heart,
   For they shall see our God;
The secret of the Lord is theirs;
   Their soul is Christ's abode.

Still to the lowly soul   **1042691**
   He doth himself impart,
And for his temple and his throne
   Selects the pure in heart.

Lord, we thy presence seek,
   May ours this blessing be:
O give the pure and lowly heart,
   A temple meet for thee!
      —JOHN KEBLE

PRAYER:

Our Father, we are thankful for the privilege of coming into thy presence. Forgive us for the times when we have held back and have not given thee a place in our lives. We are sorry for refusing to follow thy leadership. Going in our own willful way we have missed thee on many occasions. Take from us pride and selfishness and make us humble and teachable. May we ever be aware of thy presence and set aside time to commune with thee. In Jesus' name, we pray. AMEN.

LEADER:

As we hear the story "The Other Cheek," let us decide what we would do had we been in Michael's place.

STORY:

THE OTHER CHEEK

The new kid came down to the playground that afternoon. We didn't know much about him except that his folks were English and had come from Hong Kong. They had moved into one of the apartment houses facing the park where the playground was.

We were waiting for Eddie to bring his football when we saw the new boy. He was wearing a thin white shirt with short sleeves and a pair of khaki-colored shorts that hit him just above the knees.

Jerry whistled. "Will you look at that!"

We all turned and stared at him as he came toward us. I figure he was about ten, although he was a lot smaller than me, and I'm nine. He had a lot of dark hair, and when he got closer, we could see he had real long lashes, like a girl.

He smiled at us. "Hello!"

We said hello, and Bud said, "What's your name?"

"Michael," he said. "What's yours?" He had a funny, crisp way of talking.

We stood and looked at each other.

Just then Eddie ran up with his football under his arm. "OK, you guys, let's go!" Then he saw the new kid. "Who's he?"

"His name's Michael," I said.

Eddie stared at Michael. The rest of us watched, not saying anything. Everybody's scared of Eddie. He's eleven and big for his age, and he likes to fight. He can be a lot of fun as long as you play his way.

He evidently figured the kid wasn't worth bothering about. "Go on home to Mama, pretty boy. Come on, you guys."

Michael watched us, his face eager and puzzled and wistful all at once. A few minutes later I noticed him by the sand pile, watching the little kids.

Suddenly the ball we were kicking made a crazy curve and landed in the middle of the sand pile.

One of the little kids picked it up to throw it back, but Eddie pounded up to him. "Give that here!" he yelled, grabbing it so hard that the little fellow fell down.

The new boy took a clean, folded handkerchief out of his pocket and began to wipe the sand off the little boy's knees where he had skinned them. In a minute the small boy had stopped crying and was laughing up at him. Michael squatted beside him and began to rebuild the fort the football had ruined.

Eddie didn't like that. He threw the ball into the bunch of little kids again. Then, strutting a little, he started walking toward them. We knew what was coming next and slowly followed.

The new boy had picked up the ball and was standing there, waiting for Eddie to come up to him.

"All right," Eddie said. "Let's have it."

Michael held the ball out to him. "Here's your ball," he said in a friendly voice. "But you should be more careful. Some of the children might get hurt."

You could see Eddie hadn't expected that.

"Listen, smart guy, I told you to go home. Now beat it!" With a quick movement he knocked the ball out of Michael's hand.

Michael never budged.

I had never seen anybody stand up to Eddie like that. I was scared. Nobody can act like that around Eddie and get away with it.

Eddie looked at the new kid and then at the ball, which had landed a few feet away. "Pick it up!" he ordered.

Michael just looked at him.

Eddie was furious. "Are you gonna pick it up?" he challenged.

"No," the boy said.

It was suddenly terribly quiet. Eddie stood there, his mouth open. I wondered whether he was afraid. I guess he knew that was what we were all thinking, because all at once he drew back his hand and hit the new kid across the face. "That's for pretty boys who won't do what they're told," he said. "Now go home."

Michael never budged, although we could see a bright red mark spread slowly along his cheek. I wanted to yell: "Eddie, stop it! Let him alone!" But I didn't. I was afraid. Eddie was sure of himself now. He stepped back a little, doubling up his fists.

"OK, you asked for it," he said. His left shot out, but it never connected. The new kid struck up Eddie's arm with the edge of his hand. Almost before you could see what he was doing, he grabbed Eddie's arm with both hands. He pulled on it sharply, turning away from him and sort of crouching down. Eddie flew right over his head and hit the ground with a thump. Michael straightened up and turned and looked down at him. Eddie lay there astonished.

The new kid went over to him. "I'm sorry," he said in that funny, crisp voice of his. "But you did ask for it, you know. Let me help you up." He held out his hand.

Eddie looked at him; then reached up and took Michael's hand.

"Boy!" he said, "that was some trick! Could—could you show me how to do it? That's jujitsu, isn't it?"

"Yes," Michael said. "I took lessons while we were living in Hong Kong. But I couldn't teach you. It's too dangerous unless you know exactly what you're doing. You might hurt somebody terribly, you see."

Eddie looked at Michael respectfully. I guess we all did.

"I'll tell you what, though," Michael said. "I wish you'd teach me something."

"Sure!" Eddie promised eagerly. "What is it?"

Michael smiled that eager, wistful smile. "How to play football," he said. "It looks awfully exciting." [3]

LEADER:

Let us turn to the Scriptures to find light on the problem that Michael faced.

SCRIPTURE:

Ye have heard that it hath been said, An eye for an eye, and a tooth for a tooth: But I say unto you, that ye resist not evil: but whosoever shall smite thee on thy right cheek, turn to him the other also. And if any man will sue thee at the law, and take away thy coat, let him have thy cloke also. And whosoever shall compel thee to go a mile, go with him twain. Give to him that asketh thee, and from him that would borrow of thee turn not thou away. . . .

As ye would that men should do to you, do ye also to them likewise. For if ye love them which love you, what thank have ye? for sinners also love those that love them. . . . But love ye your enemies, and do good, and lend, hoping for nothing again; and your reward shall be great, and ye shall be the children of the Highest: for he is kind unto the unthankful and to the evil. [4]

POEM:

> If you've tried and have not won,
>   Never stop for crying;
> All that's great and good is done
>   Just by patient trying.
>
> Though young birds, in flying, fall,
>   Still their wings grow stronger;

And the next time they can keep
Up a little longer.

Though the sturdy oak has known
Many a blast that bowed her,
She has risen again, and grown
Loftier and prouder.

If by easy work you beat,
Who the more will prize you?
Gaining victory from defeat,
That's the test that tries you.
—PHOEBE CARY

The question of what is right has to do not only with big decisions but with all our daily living and acting.

Let us ask ourselves, "How would I like to be treated if I were in Michael's place?" From the example of Jesus we learn that he taught that all people are children of God and should be treated with respect and good will. Do we always treat all people alike?

When tempted in the wilderness, Jesus in his reply to the tempter quoted from the Scriptures, "It is written, Man shall not live by bread alone, but by every word that proceedeth out of the mouth of God." "Get thee hence, Satan: for it is written, Thou shalt worship the Lord thy God, and him only shalt thou serve."

Do we know the Bible well enough to find help with our problems? If not, more time spent in reading and studying the Bible would shed light on the choices we have to make.

At the beginning of his ministry and when choosing his disciples, Jesus spent much time in prayer. Would it not be well if we take our problems to God in prayer, asking that he reveal his will and purpose for us?

We might discuss our problems in the youth fellowship. There is no better place than in such a group to discover right attitudes and plan for Christian action.

POEM:

Gracious Spirit, dwell with me;
I myself would gracious be;
And with words that help and heal
Would thy life in mine reveal;

And with actions bold and meek
Would for Christ my Saviour speak.

Truthful Spirit, dwell with me;
I myself would truthful be;
And with wisdom kind and clear
Let thy life in mine appear;
And with actions brotherly
Speak my Lord's sincerity.

.   .   .   .

Holy Spirit, dwell with me;
I myself would holy be;
Separate from sin, I would
Choose and cherish all things good,
And whatever I can be
Give to him who gave me thee!
—THOMAS TOKE LYNCH

PRAYER:

O Lord, wilt thou guide us as we seek to know what is right; give us courage to stand for the hard right against the easy wrong. When our vision grows dim, open our eyes and help us to see what thou hast in store for us. When we lack courage, strengthen us. Reveal thy will and help us to follow thee in every thought and act of our lives. Forgive us for trying to get the best things for ourselves, instead of being quick to see that others have their share. Forgive us for hurting people and for the many chances that we have missed to be kind, considerate, and courteous to others. In the name of him who said, "I am come that they might have life, and that they might have it more abundantly," we pray. AMEN.

HYMN: "Are Ye Able" or
"March On, O Soul, With Strength"

BENEDICTION:

Lead us in the path that shineth more and more unto the perfect day. AMEN.

SERVICE 5

GOD SPEAKS THROUGH NATURE

PRELUDE: Hymn tune "Vesper hymn"

CALL TO WORSHIP:

O God our Father,
We would ascend into thy holy hill,
And stand in thy glorious presence,
That we may commune with thee;
Therefore cleanse our hands,
And purify our hearts;
And reveal thy beauty and thy truth
To guide us unto thyself. AMEN.[1]
—CHAUNCEY R. PIETY

HYMN: "Now, on Land and Sea Descending" or
"For the Beauty of the Earth"

SCRIPTURE:

O Lord, how manifold are thy works; in wisdom hast thou made them all: the earth is full of thy riches. . . .

When I consider thy heavens, the work of thy fingers, the moon and the stars, which thou hast ordained;

What is man, that thou art mindful of him? and the son of man, that thou visitest him?

For thou hast made him a little lower than the angels, and hast crowned him with glory and honour.

Thou madest him to have dominion over the works of thy hands; thou hast put all things under his feet: . . .

O Lord our Lord, how excellent is thy name in all the earth! [2]

PRAYER:

O God, thou hast made all things, the earth, the sky, the sea, the birds, the flowers, and all other living things. Thou hast made us in thine own image with the ability to understand thy will for us. Help us to see thee in the abundance that thou hast provided for us. In the beauty which thou hast provided, may we see thy goodness toward us. In all the things that enrich life may we see thy love and care for us. Increase our faith in what we may become and help us to overcome our fears and frustrations. In Jesus' name. AMEN.

LEADER:

If God watches over the birds, the lilies of the field, is it too much to expect him to watch over us? Do we feel secure in his guidance and care?

"Wherefore, if God so clothe the grass of the field, which to day is, and to morrow is cast into the oven, shall he not much more clothe you, O ye of little faith?" [3]

As we begin to see God in his creation, does it lead to a desire to know more about God? We may go on discovering more and more about God, and yet not know all about him.

POEM:

> There's a part of the sun in the apple,
>   There's a part of the moon in a rose;
> There's a part of the flaming Pleiades
>   In every leaf that grows.
>
> Out of the vast comes nearness;
>   For the God whose love we sing
> Lends a little of his heaven
>   To every living thing. [4]
>   —AUGUSTUS WRIGHT BAMBERGER

> We can only see a little of the ocean,
>   Just a few miles distant from the rocky shore;
> But out there—far beyond our eye's horizon,
>   There's more, immeasurably more.

GOD SPEAKS THROUGH NATURE

We can only see a little of God's loving—
A few rich treasures from his mighty store;
But out there—far beyond our eyes' horizon,
There's more—immeasurably more.[5]

—AUTHOR UNKNOWN

LEADER:

The hymn "O Lord, We See Thy Glory" is a new hymn that was written by Edgerton Grant for use during National Youth Week. Mr. Grant is a member of the Congregational Church.

O Lord, we see thy glory in nature's wondrous ways;
We read creation's story, and sing the Maker's praise;
But why the long contending with traitor and with thief,
And conflicts never ending? Lord, help our unbelief!

O Lord, we do adore thee, thy beauty and thy grace;
We bend the knee before thee, and long to see thy face;
But still we strive for pleasure, the joy that's all too brief,
And miss thy priceless treasure: Lord, help our unbelief!

O Lord, our lives are failing when lived apart from thee;
Our efforts unavailing till faith shall set us free.
Behold our deep desire;—thy grace we would receive;
Do thou our hearts inspire—to cry, "Lord, we believe!"[6]

—EDGERTON GRANT

LEADER:

Jean Henri Fabre, a Frenchman, found God in some of the most commonplace things he had created. We will hear the story of this man who gave most of his life to a study of insects which we usually pass by without noticing.

STORY:

FABRE SEARCHES FOR TRUTH

During his childhood Jean Henri Fabre made his home with his grandparents. They lived on a rocky farm on the coast of France where they raised sheep and cattle for a living. The boy loved the lambs but was more interested in insects. During these early years when he was free to roam the woods, he began the study that held his interest the remainder of his life.

At this time nature books contained very little about insects, for no one had taken the trouble to learn much about them. Jean Henri lay on the ground for hours watching these tiny creatures, learning their habits, and finding out how they cared for their young. He liked the bright colors of their wings, and their calls or chirps were music to him. He brought many of them home to study at close range. It was a great event when he found out something new about them. Immediately he made a record of it in his notebook, which he kept faithfully.

While teaching in a boy's school, Fabre came across a book on insects that helped him to decide on his life's work. A false statement in the book caused him to be more careful in keeping his own record. The book stated that a wasp kills beetles before bringing them home for its young to feed upon in the larvae stage. Watching the wasps he discovered that they stabbed the beetles in a nerve center and paralyzed them. Thus they were kept alive and fresh until eaten by the larvae.

Making this discovery led Fabre to want to prove everything that had been written on insects up to that time. This was a big task which took many years, but it opened up an entire new field of knowledge. As Fabre continued with his study, mysteries were cleared up and a careful record was kept of all he learned.

Fabre was so busy with his research that he made no effort to have his works printed. After many years, when others insisted that he share his knowledge, he had a few volumes printed on cheap paper. The readers were amazed at the facts revealed, and his stories had such charm that they won for him many friends. At last ten volumes were necessary in order to bring out all that he had gathered about insects.

Fame finally came to this tireless worker, but he remained poor throughout his life. He was well up in years before he owned any land, and he let it grow up in weeds and briars. When his friends spoke of this, he replied, "I am too busy to farm. All that I wanted with this land was a place to study insects."

On his eighty-seventh birthday a great event was planned to which scientists, writers, and other important people came. Many were surprised to see an elderly man living quietly on a poor farm that was infested with insects. But others saw a great observer who was still keenly interested in the small creatures to which he had given a lifetime of study. He was pleased at the gifts and honors bestowed upon him on his birthday. But his greatest happiness came when ten volumes of his writings were printed and others could learn about his discoveries.

When someone inquired, "Do you believe in God?" Fabre replied, "I see God in all things everywhere." Those who study his books find that there is a reverence for the Creator in all of his writings. He spoke of the law and order in the universe and of the wisdom of the Creator in the plans he made for the smallest and humblest insects.

POEM:

My God, I thank thee, who hast made
  The earth so bright,
So full of splendor and of joy,
  Beauty and light;
So many glorious things are here,
  Noble and right.

I thank thee, too, that thou hast made
  Joy to abound,
So many gentle thoughts and deeds
  Circling us 'round,
That in the darkest spot of earth
  Some love is found.

I thank thee, Lord, that thou hast kept
  The best in store;
We have enough, yet not too much,
  To long for more;
A yearning for a deeper peace
  Not known before.
       —ADELAIDE A. PROCTOR

POEM:

God, who touchest earth with beauty,
  Make me lovely too;
With thy spirit re-create me,
  Make my heart anew.

Like thy springs and running waters,
  Make me crystal pure;
Like thy rocks of towering grandeur,
  Make me strong and sure.

Like thy dancing waves in sunlight,
  Make me glad and free;
Like the straightness of the pine trees
  Let me upright be.

Like the arching of the heavens,
  Lift my thoughts above;
Turn my dreams to noble action—
  Ministries of love.

God, who touchest earth with beauty,
  Make me lovely too;
Keep me ever, by thy Spirit,
  Pure and strong and true.[7]

—MARY S. EDGAR

PRAYER:

Our Father, when we think of all thou hast created for our enjoyment, we are grateful for thy goodness to us. As we think of thy plans and provision for the smallest creatures, we are convinced that thou dost care for us. Reveal to us thy plan and purpose for us; show us the ways we can help to bring thy kingdom nearer. Give us patience to follow even when we can see only a part of the way. When frustration comes and the way seems long, give us courage to press on. Guide us into service activities that will help to make the world a better and happier place. In Jesus' name, we pray. AMEN.

HYMN: "This Is My Father's World" or
    "Day Is Dying in the West"

BENEDICTION:

May we go from this service with a greater desire to bring beauty into the lives of others. AMEN.

SERVICE 6

GOD SPEAKS THROUGH PATRIOTS

PRELUDE: Hymn tune "Blairgowrie"

CALL TO WORSHIP:
> Thou must be true thyself
> If thou the truth wouldst teach;
>
> . . . .
>
> Think truly, and thy thoughts
> Shall the world's famine feed;
> Speak truly, and each word of thine
> Shall be a fruitful seed;
> Live truly, and thy life shall be
> A great and noble creed.
> —HORATIUS BONAR

HYMN: "Take Thou Our Minds, Dear Lord" or
"Now in the Days of Youth"

RESPONSIVE READING:
Leader: Jesus saith unto him, I am the way, the truth, and the life.
Group: Thou art the Way: to thee alone
    From sin and death we flee;
And he who would the Father seek
    Must seek him, Lord, by thee.
Leader: Pilate saith unto him, What is truth? . . .
    To this end was I born, and for this cause came I into
the world, that I should bear witness unto the truth.

47

Group: Thou art the Truth: thy word alone
   True wisdom can impart;
   Thou only canst inform the mind,
   And purify the heart.
Leader: Ye shall know the truth, and the truth shall make you free.
Group: Thou art the Life: the rending tomb
   Proclaims thy conquering arm,
   And those who put their trust in thee
   Nor death nor hell shall harm.
Leader: I am come that they might have life, and that they might
   have it more abundantly.[1]
Group: Thou art the Way, the Truth, the Life:
   Grant us that Way to know,
   That Truth to keep, that Life to win,
   Whose joys eternal flow.

—GEORGE W. DOANE

PRAYER:

Our Father, we thank thee for health and strength and for work to
do. Help us in our daily tasks; purify our minds and strengthen our
wills, so that we may always choose what is right. AMEN.

LEADER:

We will hear the story of the patriot who wrote the Declaration of
Independence.

STORY:

A GREAT PATRIOT

As a lad Thomas Jefferson was tall and red-headed, with large
hands and feet, and seemed like an ordinary American boy. There
was nothing about his appearance that would indicate future greatness.
He was born on Shadwell plantation, in Albemarle County, Virginia,
April 13, 1743. His father was a small farmer but was capable and
industrious.

Later the Jefferson family moved to Tuckahoe, where the father
managed one of the finest plantations in the state. Thomas' early life
was spent in a center of culture in the stately manor house at Tuckahoe. Here at five years of age he started to school. One of his traits at
this time that followed him through life was his inquisitive mind. His
teacher complained, "Young Jefferson can ask more questions than

any boy I have ever known." This trait helped him to store up all sorts of knowledge.

When not in school Thomas roamed the wilderness, learning to handle a gun, swim, row, and ride horseback. He had an ideal companion in his father. What counted most were the evenings with his father, reading history and the lives of great men from the library at Tuckahoe. This started him well on his way to a life of service to his country.

When Thomas was fourteen his father died, leaving him the head of the family. Caring for his mother and two sisters caused him to grow up faster than most boys. Moving back to Shadwell the boy went to a private school taught by the Rev. James Maury. Three pupils in this school became presidents of the United States—James Madison, James Monroe, and Thomas Jefferson.

Thomas spent his free time with Dabney Carr, who later married his sister. The boys often rode to the top of a nearby hill from which there was a splendid view. Young Jefferson said, "When I grow up, I am going to build a beautiful home on this hilltop." This dream came true when he built Monticello, one of the famous homes of this country, on that spot.

At seventeen Thomas entered William and Mary College at Williamsburg, where he made close friends of many of the leaders. Governor Fauquier invited him to his home to play violin duets with him. George Wythe, a prominent lawyer, was attracted to the lively boy who played classical music with men twice his age.

The years spent at Williamsburg had a great influence upon the tall, awkward boy. He was thrilled by speeches made by Patrick Henry on freedom and justice. Studying in the law office of George Wythe gave him a chance to put his thoughts in writing and prepare for the tasks ahead. During seven years of law practice he discussed the questions that were in the minds of the leaders at that time.

Jefferson gave up his law practice because of the Revolution. In 1779 he was elected governor of Virginia and after serving two years was sent as minister to France. Upon his return he was secretary of state in Washington's cabinet and vice-president in John Adams' cabinet.

In 1801 Jefferson was elected President of the United States and served two terms. He doubled the size of our country by buying from Napoleon the section west of the Mississippi River to the Rockies. Some thought him extravagant because he paid three cents an acre for this rich land. From English currency he changed our system to dollars and cents.

At the close of his second term he went to Monticello to live but always kept up his interest in public affairs. Many of his inventions may be seen in this mansion today—the dumb waiter, private stairways, tunnels, an outdoor clock, and a machine for writing duplicate letters. He loved women, children, and flowers, and enjoyed having his friends at his home. At Dabney Carr's death he brought his sister and her children to his home, where he cared for them.

Jefferson's greatest service was to write the Declaration of Independence. A committee of five was asked to write it, but he was the author, for he put it in its final form. After working two days he read it to Congress, where it was debated and passed on July 4, 1776. He believed in equal opportunities for all and that light and liberty are on a steady advance and would come in all countries. Throughout his life he struggled for the rights and freedom we enjoy today. He passed away on July 4, 1826, fifty years after signing the Declaration of Independence.

POEM:

> I live for those who love me,
>   Whose hearts are kind and true;
> For the Heaven that smiles above me,
>   And awaits my spirit too;
> For all human ties that bind me,
> For the task by God assigned me,
> For the bright hopes yet to find me,
>   And the good that I can do.
>
> I live to learn their story
>   Who suffered for my sake;
> To emulate their glory
>   And follow in their wake:
> Bards, patriots, martyrs, sages,
> The heroic of all ages,
> Whose deeds crowd History's pages
>   And Time's great volume make.
>
> I live to hold communion
>   With all that is divine,

GOD SPEAKS THROUGH PATRIOTS

To feel there is a union
  'Twixt Nature's heart and mine;
To profit by affliction,
Reap truth from fields of fiction,
Grow wiser from conviction,
  And fulfill God's grand design.
      —G. LINNAEUS BANKS

POEM:

Great truths are greatly won. Not found by chance,
Nor wafted on the breath of summer dream,
But grasped in the great struggle of the soul,
Hard buffeting with adverse wind and stream,
Wrung from the troubled spirit in hard hours
Of weakness, solitude, perchance of pain,
Truth springs, like harvest, from the well-plowed field,
And the soul feels it has not wept in vain.
      —HORATIUS BONAR

PRAYER:

Our Father, we thank thee for patriots who put self in the background and worked for the good of their country. May we cherish the ideals on which our nation was founded and strive to live by them. Give us faith and courage to work for a better world in which there will be freedom, justice, and peace for all nations. Forgive our personal and national sins and hasten the day when we learn to live together as brothers. We ask it in Jesus' name. AMEN.

HYMN: "Rise Up, O Men of God" or
      "Once to Every Man and Nation"

BENEDICTION:

Dismiss us with thy blessing and guide us in ways of peace and right living. AMEN.

SERVICE 7

GOD SPEAKS THROUGH CRUSADERS

PRELUDE: Hymn tune "National Hymn"

CALL TO WORSHIP:

> Our Fathers' God to thee
> Author of liberty,
> To thee we sing:
> Long may our land be bright,
> With freedom's holy light;
> Protect us by thy might,
> Great God our King.
>
> —SAMUEL F. SMITH

HYMN: "Heralds of Christ, Who Bear the King's Commands" or "God of Our Fathers, Whose Almighty Hand"

SCRIPTURE:

> O send out thy light and thy truth: let them lead me;
> Let them bring me unto thy holy hill, . . .
> When he, the Spirit of truth, is come,
> He will guide you into all truth: . . .
> Righteousness exalteth a nation: but sin is a reproach
>   to any people. . . .
> Blessed is the nation whose God is the Lord.[1]

AFFIRMATION OF BELIEF:

> I believe in man,
> Made a little lower than God,

Crowned with glory and honor,
And given dominion over the earth.

I believe in man,
Created spiritually like God,
With a mind that hungers for truth,
With a heart that loves good more than evil,
With a dynamic will that dares to do,
And with a boundless capacity for growth and progress.

I believe in man,
Who dreamed and prayed and planned,
And from the jungle built the world we know;
And being conscious of present evils,
He still dreams and struggles and prays
To build integrity, justice, good will, brotherhood
    and everlasting peace.
I believe in man, the offspring of God,
Potentially and eventually triumphant.[2]

—CHAUNCEY R. PIETY

PRAYER:
Our Father, we are grateful for the founders of our nation, for their ideals. Help us to make their faith our faith. Bless those who rule over us and guide our nation. Lead us in paths of peace and justice; fill our hearts with love and lead us in the paths of service. Help us to be Christian patriots who live together in a spirit of brotherhood. In Jesus' name, we pray. AMEN.

LEADER:
We still hear the story of a man who lived over 250 years ago. His memory still lives, and he seems more real to us than many other more recent leaders.

STORY:

BENJAMIN FRANKLIN, A CRUSADER

Benjamin Franklin, the youngest son of seventeen children, was born in Boston, January 17, 1706. Though he quit school at ten years of age, he was a student all his life. His first work was helping his father, a candlemaker, and later his brother, a printer.

The boy loved the sea and wanted to be a sailor, but instead became a printer. To him printing was more than a job—it was a means of spreading truth and knowledge. He had wide interests and worked at many things but always spoke of himself as a printer.

Benjamin was hardly started at his trade when his brother was thrown into prison for criticising local leaders in his newspaper. Though only sixteen years of age, Benjamin brought out the next issues of the paper. Knowing that these leaders would watch closely the column of the paper, the lad took up the fight that his brother had started and gave his own ideas on free speech.

Benjamin stated that, when men differed in their opinions, both sides should be heard and that, when truth and error had fair play, truth would win out. Thus he began the fight for freedom that lasted throughout his long life. His crusade had a great influence on others and helped our country to gain its freedom.

A year later when the boy could not see much future in working for his brother, he went to Philadelphia, where he worked for another printer. When ready to set up his own printing plant, he made a trip to England to buy type and supplies. Staying long enough to work with some of the best printers, he learned much of their skill.

Returning home Franklin turned out some of the finest printing of any shop in America, and in a short while he had more than his share of the work. His business expanded until he was the largest consumer of paper in the country.

At twenty-three years of age Franklin printed the first novel in America, the first illustrated newspaper story, and the first cartoon. His *Poor Richard's Almanac* was so popular that it was translated into twelve languages and widely read in many countries. His best-known book today is his *Autobiography*.

Franklin studied medicine and experimented with electricity. He organized the first circulating library, the first police force, the first fire department, and the first hospital in Philadelphia. He invented the bifocal lens, the Franklin stove, and many other useful objects. A school that he founded later became the University of Pennsylvania.

Living at a time when Great Britain was having trouble with her colonies, Franklin was twice sent to England as a diplomat. He was successful for some time in working out better relations between England and the American colonies. But when the situation became critical, he came home and threw himself into the Revolution. Later as a minister to France he secured aid from the French that helped the Colonies to win in their fight against Great Britain. He also worked out treaties with Sweden and Prussia. He is considered one of our greatest diplomats.

Franklin is the only man in this country who signed four of its most important papers—the Declaration of Independence, the Constitution, the Treaty with France, and the Treaty with Great Britain. Without even one of these documents our country could not have been the great country that it is today. Few people have been successful in so many fields and still had the honor and respect of their fellow men.

Franklin often expressed thanks to God for his providence that had brought him success along the way. When the freedoms for which he had worked were taking shape, he expressed the desire that people of all nations might have the same privileges that we enjoy. He held to the idea that people who work for freedom are in the right and may expect God's help. The freedoms that we enjoy today are largely the result of the crusade for human rights that he led.

POEM:

> God bless our native land!
> Firm may she ever stand,
>   Through storm and night:
> When the wild tempests rave,
> Ruler of wind and wave,
> Do thou our country save
>   By thy great might!
>
> For her our prayer shall rise
> To God, above the skies;
>   On him we wait:
> Thou who art ever nigh,
> Guarding with watchful eye,
> To thee aloud we cry,
>   God save the state!
>
> Not for this land alone,
> But be God's mercies shown
>   From shore to shore;
> And may the nations see
> That men should brothers be,
> And form one family
>   The wide world o'er.
>   —SIEGFRIED A. MAHLMANN

Let us pledge allegiance to the flag of our country:

"I pledge allegiance to the flag of the United States of America and to the republic for which it stands; one nation under God, indivisible, with liberty and justice for all."

Let us salute the Christian flag:

"I pledge allegiance to the Christian flag and to the Savior for whose kingdom it stands: one brotherhood, uniting all mankind in service and love."

PRAYER:

Our Father, we are grateful for leaders like Franklin who helped to make our country free. Keep us humble and may we be willing to learn from the example of others. Make us patient, willing to forgive; grant us wisdom to know what is right and give us courage to follow it. Help us to appreciate the freedom that has come to us and may we guard it carefully. Give us patience to run the race that is before us, forgetting the things that are behind, reaching out for the things that are before, so that at last we may find eternal life. AMEN.

HYMN: "Rise up, O men of God"
        "March on, O Soul, with Strength"

BENEDICTION:

Thy spirit be within us until nations shall learn to dwell together in peace through their love for thee. AMEN.

SERVICE 8

GOD SPEAKS THROUGH FRIENDS

PRELUDE: Hymn tune "Amesbury"

CALL TO WORSHIP:
>   The Lord is in his holy temple; [1]
>   Let all the earth keep silence before him.

HYMN: "Awake, Awake to Love and Work" or
      "When Morning Gilds the Sky"

SCRIPTURE:
Then one of them, which was a lawyer, asked him a question, tempting him, and saying, Master, which is the great commandment in the law? Jesus said unto him, Thou shalt love the Lord thy God with all thy heart, and with all thy soul, and with all thy mind. This is the first and great commandment. And the second is like unto it, Thou shalt love thy neighbour as thyself. On these two commandments hang all the law and the prophets. . . . A new commandment I give unto you, That ye love one another; as I have loved you, that ye also love one another. By this shall all men know that ye are my disciples, if ye have love one to another. . . .

Love is patient and kind; love is not jealous or boastful; it is not arrogant or rude. Love does not insist on its own way; it is not irritable or resentful; it does not rejoice at wrong, but rejoices in the right. Love bears all things, believes all things, hopes all things, endures all things. Love never ends. [2]

POEM:

> For all the blessings of the year,
> For all the friends we hold so dear,
> For peace on earth, both far and near,
>   We thank thee, Lord.
>
> For life and health, those common things,
> Which every day and hour brings,
> For home, where our affection clings,
>   We thank thee, Lord.
>
> For love of thine, which never tires,
> Which all our better thought inspires,
> And warms our lives with heavenly fires,
>   We thank thee, Lord.
>   —ALBERT H. HUTCHINSON

LEADER:

In the story that you will hear Doak Walker tells us about what his friends have meant to him.

STORY:

EVERY KID HAS HIS HERO

Doak Walker

As a boy I had my heroes. One was Harry Shuford, a great triple threat star for Southern Methodist from 1933-1935. In grade school English class I wrote a theme about Harry, who, I pointed out, was great not only because of his ability, but because he had ideals and gave up individual honors to boost his teammates. I wanted to be like Harry.

My dad has always been a hero to me. As football coach at North Dallas High, he started tossing a football at me when I was 18 months old. When I was 3, I made my first trip to the high school locker room and immediately fell in love with the leathery, sweaty, locker-room odors. . . . At the age of 6 I had learned to drop kick a ball over the clothesline in our backyard. . . . There was plenty of time for athletics in my young world, but my parents made it clear to me that sports were not the most important thing in life.

God had top spot in our family. . . . Both mother and dad taught Sunday school in the Westminster Presbyterian church. I can well remember slipping out of my junior Sunday school room and into my father's class for older boys . . . to listen intently to his down-to-earth interpretation of Christian living.

Since it wasn't possible for me to have dad as my high school football coach, then I'm glad it was Rusty Russell. Rusty not only built strong teams, but his coaching program was aimed at promoting ideals and creating lifelong friendships. One fall he had us camp together in the gym for two weeks before school opened. We practiced on the field, ate together in the school cafeteria and slept in the gym camp style.

It was during one of these nights that our squad got together and spent a lot of time and thought working out a set of football objectives. The seven rules we drew up included emphasis on sportsmanship, hard but fair play, learning to think, personal conduct on and off the field, knowing how to take defeat and the importance of scholarship.

Bobby Layne and I were co-captains of our high school team that year. Bobby, one of the closest friends I ever had, went on to Texas University. A year later I went to Southern Methodist.

The college game which I will perhaps remember longer than any other was the one we played against each other back in 1947 in the Cotton Bowl. At game time both Texas and SMU were undefeated and untied. Bobby and I had been playing together since Junior High; now we would have a chance to match wits against each other in friendly rivalry. Layne had already become recognized nationally as one of the best passers in the game.

Texas kicked off to us. In a few quick plays we scored a touchdown and led 7-0. Then Bobby got his passing wizardry going and it was soon 7-7. Later in the game we scored again and kicked the point to make it 14-7. Bobby's passes netted another touchdown, but the all-important extra point was missed. We won 14-13.

It was one of those very exciting, rugged, but clean games that make competitive sports so stimulating for youth. Victories are wonderful, . . . but you can't win them all, and the defeats, believe me, are good in teaching humility. . . .

Every man has a right to work out his own life pattern and personal convictions. I have never been ashamed of my complete faith in God. It means too much to me. I do not drink, . . . therefore, it was no problem for me to turn down a $50,000 radio offer from a beer sponsor. I don't see how alcoholic drinks can help me get any more fun and satisfaction out of life than I do now.

I wouldn't be human if I didn't say that I've loved the excitement of football. But the things that have meant most in the long run are the friendships gained, the sense of values learned, and the hope that perhaps in some way I've measured up to my boyhood idol, Harry Shuford.[3]

POEM:

> If you walk as a friend you will find a friend,
> Wherever you choose to fare,
> If you go with mirth to a far strange land
> You will find that mirth is there,
> For the strangest part of this queer old world
> Is that like will join with like;
> And who walks with love for his fellow man,
> An answering love will strike.
>
> If you walk in honor, then honest men
> Will meet you along the way,
> But if you are false you will find men false
> Wherever you chance to stray.
> For good breeds good and bad breeds bad,
> We are met by the traits we show,
> Love will find a friend at the stranger's door,
> Where hate will find a foe.
>
> For each of us builds the world he knows,
> Which only himself can spoil,
> And an hour of hate or an hour of shame
> Can ruin a life of toil,
> And though to the utmost ends of the earth
> Your duty may bid you fare,
> If you go with truth and a friendly heart,
> You will find friends waiting there.
>
> —AUTHOR UNKNOWN

LEADER:

When we hear that someone did a courageous, heroic act, does it remind us of one we admire and does it lead us to want to build into our lives the same reactions? Let us list on the blackboard some characteristics that we would like to build into our lives, putting the most important ones first.

GOD SPEAKS THROUGH FRIENDS

POEM:

> Almighty Lord, with one accord
> We offer Thee our youth,
> And pray that Thou wouldst give us now
> The warfare of the truth.
>
> Thy cause doth claim our souls by name,
> Because that we are strong;
> In all the land, one steadfast band,
> May we to Christ belong.
>
> Let fall on ev'ry college hall
> The luster of Thy cross,
> That love may dare Thy work to share
> And count all else as loss.
>
> Our hearts be ruled, our spirits schooled
> Alone Thy will to seek;
> And when we find Thy blessed mind,
> Instruct our lips to speak.
> —M. WOOLSEY STRYKER

HYMN: "I Would Be True" or
"Give of Your Best"

PRAYER:
Our Father, we thank thee for the gift of friendship and for the friends who have enriched our lives and have encouraged us. Forbid that we should ever draw a circle and shut out any who need friends. If we have been busy, thinking only of ourselves, forgive us. We are grateful for the power that love has to drive selfishness out of our hearts. Help us to be more worthy of our friends. Guide us in our friendships and lead us to a closer companionship with thee. In Jesus' name we pray. AMEN.

BENEDICTION:
May the love and peace of Christ abide in our hearts in the days ahead. AMEN.

SERVICE 9

GOD SPEAKS THROUGH PEACEMAKERS

PRELUDE: "Serenade" by Schubert

CALL TO WORSHIP:
>Let the people praise thee, ...
>O let the nations be glad and sing for joy:
>For thou shalt judge the people righteously,
>And govern the nations upon earth.[1]

HYMN: "He Leadeth Me" or
>"Breathe on Me, Breath of God"

SCRIPTURE:
And many nations shall come, and say, Come, and let us go up to the mountain of the Lord, and to the house of the God of Jacob; and he will teach us of his ways, and we will walk in his paths: ... And he shall judge among many people, and rebuke strong nations afar off; and they shall beat their swords into plowshares, and their spears into pruninghooks: nation shall not lift up a sword against nation, neither shall they learn war any more. ...

Mark the perfect man, and behold the upright: for the end of that man is peace. ...

Blessed are the peacemakers: for they shall be called the children of God.[2]

POEM:
>God of our boyhood, whom we yield
>The tribute of our youthful praise,

62

Upon the well-contested field,
And 'mid the glory of these days,
God of our youth, be with us yet,
Lest we forget, lest we forget.

Sturdy of limb, with bounding health,
Eager to play the hero's part,
Grant to us each that greater wealth—
An undefiled and loyal heart,
God of our youth, be thou our might,
To do the right, to do the right.

—AUTHOR UNKNOWN

LEADER:

We will hear the story of William Penn, who pioneered in peaceful ways of living.

STORY:

WILLIAM PENN, A PIONEER IN PEACE

William Penn, born in London, spent his childhood in the country, where he enjoyed the out-of-doors. His interest in sports helped him to build a strong body. He studied in Chigwell School, where he was given Puritan training. At the age of sixteen he entered Christ Church College, Oxford, where he spent two unhappy years. His Puritan background made the gay life at college seem frivolous. The students thought him queer and avoided him because he was serious and studied much of the time.

Later William was sent to Lamur College, where he made friends of the Quakers. This new sect was unpopular largely because they would not fight or take an oath under any circumstance. The young man was attracted to these quiet people who harmed no one and yet were persecuted. He liked their worship largely because everyone was free to talk to God about his own problems. During his vacation he studied their beliefs.

As young Penn met with the Quakers, he wondered why everyone could not live peaceably as they did, why people could not worship God in their own way without persecution, and why Christians did not try to correct some of the evils that hindered worship. The Quakers' way of listening quietly to God and their sincere effort to follow the ideas coming to them seemed very good to William. He

63

accepted their beliefs and found an inward peace and inspiration in their meetings.

A strong friendship grew up between Penn and George Fox, the founder of the Quakers, or Society of Friends, group. They visited Holland and Germany together and won many converts to their way of thinking.

Penn wrote an article criticizing the Church of England for persecuting the Quakers. Instead of bringing about a change, he himself was thrown into prison. He then made a study of law in order to defend the rights of Quakers. Many of their group had been thrown into prison for minor offenses.

It was then that Penn realized that many of his ideas were far ahead of his day. At once he turned his thoughts toward America, where new ideas could be tried out without persecution. There Quakers could worship God as they pleased without having to serve prison terms.

Penn's father, a noted English admiral, had commanded the fleet against Spanish possessions in America. At his death a tract of land in America was given to William in payment for a debt that Great Britain owed his father. The territory was nearly as large as England and covered what is now Pennsylvania. From his father's estate he also received an income, which gave him the means to settle a colony of Quakers in America.

In 1681 when the charter was signed and the tract of land was set aside for the colony, an important goal was reached. There were many who were eager to come to America in search of freedom. Penn and George Fox worked out the details of the plan for the colony. As governor of the colony Penn would be fair and honest in his dealings. Unlike others, his purpose was not to build a fortune for himself but to provide a place where people could worship God as their conscience dictated.

All of the other American colonies had frequent raids and massacres by the Indians. This was probably because of unfair treatment that the Indians received from the white people. In order to avoid war, Penn called the Indian chieftains to meet with him. He paid them for their land and assured them that he wanted nothing except their friendship and good will. He promised that no harm would come to any of them or to their property from any member of his colony. The Indians agreed to keep peace. No oaths were taken, but the promises were kept by both sides.

Penn's colony was the only one that had no forts, cannons, or soldiers, and yet during the entire time of his rule not one drop of Quaker blood was shed by the Indians. He won the friendship of the warlike Indians and maintained peace between them and his colony. He also won the respect and admiration of the people of many countries because of this forward step in outlawing war.

Many of Penn's ideas were far ahead of his day. He suggested a League of Nations for Europe two hundred years before the world got around to trying out the idea. Today England honors him for the reforms that he brought about. In America he is remembered as one who lived peaceably with the hostile Indians and won them to ways of peace with love, friendship, and good will.

Poem:

> The grass grows slowly up the hill
> With faith the torrent cannot kill,
> And rocks are rough, and still the clover
> The stony fields will yet run over—
> And I know nothing that the true,
> The good, the gentle cannot do.
>
> Woodlands that the winters sadden
> The leaves of Spring again will gladden;
> And so must life forever be—
> The gentle hands work patiently
> And yet accomplish more forever
> Than these too strong or those too clever.
>
> So toils an undiscouraged God
> And covers barren fields with sod,
> And so will hate and sin surrender
> To faith still strong and love still tender—
> And I know nothing that the true,
> The good, the gentle cannot do.
>
> —Author unknown

Prayer:

Our Father, we thank thee for such men as William Penn, who pioneered in ways of love and peace and won warlike Indians by kindness and friendship. Help us to realize that love is the greatest force in the world. May we not become discouraged but overcome fear and plant in its place faith and trust that will bring about a more abundant life. Help us to realize that all men of every race and condition of life are thy children and of infinite worth. May we put out of our lives any attitudes that are contrary to thy will. Fill our hearts with kindness and consideration for all people. In the name of the Prince of Peace, we pray. AMEN.

HYMN: "Spirit of God, Descend upon My Heart" or
        "Be Thou My Vision"

BENEDICTION:
    May the peace of God, which passeth all understanding, guard our hearts and thoughts in Christ Jesus. AMEN.

GOD IN OUR LIVES

SERVICE 10

SEEK AND YOU WILL FIND

PRELUDE: Hymn tune "Palestrina"

CALL TO WORSHIP:
> Surely the Lord is in this place; . . .
> This is none other but the house of God,
> And this is the gate of heaven.
> O come, let us worship and bow down:
> Let us kneel before the Lord our Maker.[1]

HYMN: "O Son of Man, Thou Madest Known" or
"We Would See Jesus"

INVOCATION:
O God, grant us a sense of thy presence as we wait before thee. Create within us a clean heart and renew a right spirit before thee. Take from us all low desires and teach us thy will and purpose for us. In Jesus' name. AMEN.

RESPONSIVE READING:
Leader: How amiable are thy tabernacles, O Lord of hosts!
> My soul longeth, yea, even fainteth for the courts of the
> Lord; my heart and my flesh crieth out for the living God.
Group: Yea, the sparrow hath found a house, and the swallow a
> nest for herself, where she may lay her young, even thine
> altars, O Lord of hosts, my King, and my God.
Leader: Blessed are they that dwell in thy house: they will be still
> praising thee. . . .

Group: For a day in thy courts is better than a thousand. I had
rather be a doorkeeper in the house of my God, than to
dwell in the tents of wickedness. . . .

Leader: They that wait upon the Lord shall renew their strength;

Group: They shall mount up with wings as eagles; they shall run,
and not be weary; and they shall walk, and not faint.[2]

OFFERTORY:

"Bring ye all the tithes into the storehouse, that there may be meat
in mine house, and prove me now herewith, saith the Lord of hosts,
if I will not open you the windows of heaven, and pour you out a
blessing, that there shall not be room enough to receive it." [3]

In our offering today we have the privilege of sharing in the support
of youth projects around the world.

OFFERING

LEADER:

Have you ever wondered what Jesus was like when he was a youth?
In the following poem the author pictures Jesus at the time of his
visit to the Temple at Jerusalem.

POEM:

> Did Jesus come singing over the hill
>   In his thirteenth spring in Palestine?
> Did his shout, like a rain from heaven, fill
>   The boughs of orchards of olive and pine?
>
> Did the Temple burst on his boyish view
>   Like a marble flower on history's stem
> As his vision loosened its wing and flew
>   O'er the roofs and walls of Jerusalem?
>
> Did his feet go racing down the slope,
>   As his glad eyes burned toward an open gate?
> Was his young heart charged with a boundless hope?
>   Did his thoughts leap, eager and passionate? [4]
>   —HENRY GREEN BARNETT

LEADER:

Luke gives in his Gospel an incident in the life of Jesus at this time.

SEEK AND YOU WILL FIND

SCRIPTURE:

And it came to pass, that after three days they found him in the temple, sitting in the midst of the doctors, both hearing them, and asking them questions. And all that heard him were astonished at his understanding and answers. And when they saw him, they were amazed: and his mother said unto him, Son, why hast thou thus dealt with us? behold, thy father and I have sought thee sorrowing. And he said unto them, How is it that ye sought me? wist ye not that I must be about my Father's business? And they understood not the saying which he spake unto them. And he went down with them, and came to Nazareth, and was subject unto them: but his mother kept all these sayings in her heart. And Jesus increased in wisdom and stature, and in favour with God and man.

STORY:

THE BOY JESUS IN THE TEMPLE

From many sections of the country the Jewish people gathered in Jerusalem to celebrate the Passover, the greatest of their holidays. This feast was kept in memory of the time when Moses led them out of slavery in Egypt to a free country of their own. Every year as the feast was observed, they looked back to that time their forefathers had eaten in haste before leaving Egypt. As the families gathered around the table, they ate the same kind of meal—roast lamb, bitter herbs, and unleavened bread. The meal was eaten reverently in memory of that first Passover.

It was springtime when Joseph and Mary made the long trip to the Holy City to observe the Passover. In fellowship with relatives and friends, camping at night under the stars, they came at last to the Mount of Olives. Here they paused to look across the valley at the beautiful Temple on the hill. The sacred city in all its splendor stood before them. No doubt they repeated a psalm that other pilgrims used on such occasions. They would camp that night within the gates of the city and be at the Temple early the next morning.

Every Jewish boy dreamed of the time when he could go to Jerusalem and worship at the Temple. According to an ancient custom a boy could not sit with the men until he was twelve years of age. At last Jesus was old enough to worship with the men at the Temple. No doubt he came to the sacred city with high hopes and with great expectation. He wanted to remember everything that happened. He must have felt at home here and very close to God.

Questions that had not been answered in the synagogue at home probably came into Jesus' mind. Perhaps the learned men at the Temple could answer these questions. The boy may have asked questions about his Father's work and his place in it. After listening to the teachers, he may have seen more clearly what he should do. He would go back to Nazareth to live these truths in daily life. What a thrilling experience for a boy at twelve years of age to keep the Passover in the Holy City!

When the feast was over, Joseph and Mary left Jerusalem with the little group from Nazareth. Jesus lingered in the Temple listening to the teachers. The time went by so rapidly that he did not miss his family. At the close of the day when his parents were ready to make camp for the night, they noticed that he was not with the group as they had supposed.

During the day the parents had talked of the events of the past days, and it did not seem strange that they had not seen Jesus. But when they made inquiries and no one had seen him, they were alarmed. Hurrying back to Jerusalem, searching everywhere, they found him in the Temple among the teachers, listening to them and asking questions.

Jesus' mother had been so anxious that when she saw him she asked, "Why have you treated us so? Your father and I have been looking for you anxiously." The boy was surprised that they did not know where to find him. He replied, "How is it that you sought me? Did you not know that I must be in my Father's house?"

The boy did not want to worry his parents, but he had become so interested when the teachers answered his questions that he lost track of time. He had stayed behind, not to enjoy the beauty of the Temple, but to learn about his Father's work. Perhaps God's purpose for his life was made plainer to him. He would go back now with a job to do.

> O Carpenter of Nazareth,
>   Builder of life divine,
> Who shapest man to God's own law,
>   Thyself the fair design:
> Build us a tower of Christlike height,
>   That we the land may view,
> And see, like thee, our noblest work
>   Our Father's work to do.

SEEK AND YOU WILL FIND

O Thou who dost the vision send
  And givest each his task,
And with the task sufficient strength:
  Show us thy will, we ask;
Give us a conscience bold and good;
  Give us a purpose true,
That it may be our highest joy,
  Our Father's work to do.[5]
           —JAY T. STOCKING

HYMN: "O Son of Man, Our Hero Strong and Tender" or
  "More Love to Thee, O Christ"

POEM:

O Master Workman of the race,
  Thou Man of Galilee,
Who with eyes of early youth
  Eternal things did see:
We thank thee for thy boyhood faith
  That shone thy whole life through;
"Did ye not know it is my work
  My Father's work to do?"

PRAYER:

Our Father, we thank thee for all the good things coming to us
from thy bountiful hand, for the Church with its glorious past, for
the Bible with its teaching and the record of those who lived close to
thee. We thank thee for the privilege of communion with thee. We
remember that Jesus said, My house shall be called a house of prayer.
May we resolve to make it so for his name's honor and glory. Grant
us wisdom and courage to follow the example of Jesus in every choice
we make. Help us to worship thee not only with our lips but in all we
do or say. May we recognize thee as the source of all good and trust
thee to guide us. In Jesus' name. AMEN.

BENEDICTION:

Dismiss us with thy blessing and lead us into fuller living. AMEN.

SERVICE 11

WE WOULD SEE JESUS

PRELUDE

CALL TO WORSHIP:

> We would see Jesus, lo! his star is shining
> Above the stable while the angels sing;
> There in a manger on the hay reclining,
> Haste, let us lay our gifts before the King.[1]
>
> —J. EDGAR PARK

HYMN: "The Hidden Years at Nazareth!" or
"O Master Workman of the Race"

RESPONSIVE READING:

Leader: What do we know of the boyhood of Jesus from the writers of the gospels?

Group: And the child grew and became strong, filled with wisdom; and the favor of God was upon him. . . . And he went down with them and came to Nazareth, and was obedient to them.

Leader: Mention a part of the Bible that every Jewish child was taught.

Group: Every one was taught the Shema: "Hear, O Israel: The Lord our God is one Lord; and you shall love the Lord your God with all your heart, and with all your soul, and with all your might."

Every child learned the ten commandments:
"You shall have no other gods before me.
You shall not make for yourself a graven image. . . .

74

You shall not take the name of the Lord your God in vain. . . .
Observe the Sabbath day, to keep it holy, . . .
Honor your father and your mother, . . .
You shall not kill.
Neither shall you commit adultery.
Neither shall you steal.
Neither shall you bear false witness against your neighbor.
Neither shall you covet.

Leader: Mention a psalm that Jesus might have sung in the worship in the synagogue.

Group: The heavens are telling the glory of God; and the firmament proclaims his handiwork.

Day to day pours forth speech, and night to night declares knowledge.

There is no speech, nor are there words; their voice is not heard;

Yet their voice goes out through all the earth, and their words to the end of the world.[2]

Leader: In the following poem a picture is given of the attitude of boys and girls toward Jesus.

POEM:

> They knew him—everywhere he went.
> They understood the look he sent
> Straight to each young heart. Shy, or bold,
> They ran to him. He let them hold
> His strong, warm hand; he was their friend;
> He laughed with them, and he would bend
> His head to catch the least one's word;
> They knew he cared, they knew he heard.
>
> They followed him, tall girls and boys;
> He understood their grief, their joys.
> Not one—Judean, Roman, Greek,
> Or Galilean, came to seek
> His sympathy, but he could read
> Unspoken thought, unconscious need.
> They were his friends—the living sign,
> And promise of a love divine.[3]
>
> —EDITH KENT BATTLE

75

STORY:

THE BOY OF NAZARETH

What was Jesus like when he was a boy growing up in Nazareth? In our imagination we picture him strong, with firm muscles, tall and straight. His eyes were kind and sensitive to the beauty about him. He lived much in the open—perhaps with shepherds as they watched their sheep, with fishermen as they supplied food for their families, or with farmers as they sowed the seed and harvested the grain.

We think of Jesus helping Joseph in the carpenter shop, taking simple tasks at first and later doing a man's work. When he made a yoke for an ox, it was smooth; his cabinets were beautiful as well as useful; his chairs were sturdy and comfortable. We picture him helping his mother with the work about the home. He knew about yeast in the dough, patching a worn garment, and sweeping the floor to find a coin.

We believe that Jesus understood nature's ways. A storm did not frighten him; he knew about the seasons, wind, rain, and sunshine. He spoke of birds, flowers, grape vines, fig trees, and grass. He knew what happened when seed fell on different kinds of soil. He noticed that a tiny mustard seed grew into a plant large enough for birds to rest on its branches. He knew the danger that lurked in the caves on the hillsides near his home.

We like to remember Jesus growing up in a happy family, loving his parents, brothers, and sisters. We picture him helping with the work and after work hours playing with the same zest. His brothers and sisters may have followed him around to hear him talk and listen to his stories. He was never too busy to lend a hand when help was needed. Being the oldest brother, he helped take care of the younger ones, which was not always an easy task.

Jesus went to school with other boys of Nazareth. He read from parts of the Bible that we call the Old Testament—the stories of Abraham, Isaac, David, Moses, and Joseph. On the Sabbath he went to the synagogue and heard other parts of the sacred writings read.

Jesus knew of God's promise to send a leader who would deliver the people from their distress and make of them a great nation. He began to think much about this Deliverer and wonder when he would come.

WE WOULD SEE JESUS

We would see Jesus, Mary's Son most holy,
　　Light of the village life from day to day;
Shining revealed through every task most lowly,
　　The Christ of God, the Life, the Truth, the Way.

We would see Jesus, on the mountain teaching,
　　With all the listening people gathered round;
While birds and flowers and sky above are preaching
　　The blessedness which simple trust has found[4]

　　　　　　　　　　　　　　—J. Edgar Park

Story:

JESUS BEGINS HIS MINISTRY

Jesus grew up in Nazareth in the north, and his cousin John lived to the south. John was preaching at the ford of Jordan, saying that the kingdom of God was about to come. The people were asking, "Are you the Messiah?" He replied, "No, I am preparing the way for the Messiah, trying to get the people ready for his coming."

Jesus came to the Jordan asking John to baptize him. As soon as he came, John knew that he was the one about whom he had been preaching. He said to the people, "Behold the Lamb of God." John did not feel worthy to baptize one so great. But Jesus wanted to show that he had joined the rest of the people in their hopes for the coming of the Kingdom.

As John baptized him, Jesus felt the approval of God. He knew that divine power would be given him to do his work. He went into the wilderness to think and to pray, to find God's plan for his work. To all the temptations he said, "No." He wanted only to do God's will.

Back in Galilee Jesus called some men to be his followers. He said to them, "Follow me, and I will make you fishers of men." Jesus preached in towns and villages, saying, "The kingdom of heaven is at hand."

What was Jesus like during his ministry? From the Bible we learn that the common people heard him gladly. He had sympathy for the poor, the outcast, the handicapped. In his own home it had not been easy to provide food and clothing for a large family. He understood the problems of the poor.

The crowds flocked to hear Jesus. During days that were filled with teaching he took time to heal the sick, give sight to the blind, and to minister to each according to his need. When mothers brought little children to him, the disciples wanted to send them away, but Jesus took them in his arms and blessed them.

There were enemies who tried to trap Jesus with difficult questions, but he was too shrewd for them. His reply showed an insight into truth that they could not fail to see. He always forgave the sinner who was ready to turn from his evil ways. His worst criticism was for those who were bad but who pretended to be good.

In his daily life Jesus showed how to live as brothers with all people, to love instead of hate, to lift the fallen, and to strengthen the weak. He found his Father's plan for his life, preached the good news of the kingdom of heaven, challenged the customs that were wrong, and shared his vision with the disciples and others who followed him. In common everyday tasks he showed how life can be lived at its best in any situation.

POEM:

We would see Jesus, in his work of healing,
    At eventide before the sun was set;
Divine and human, in his deep revealing
    Of God and man in loving service met.

We would see Jesus, in the early morning
    Still as of old he calleth, "Follow me";
Let us arise, all meaner service scorning,
    Lord, we are thine, we give ourselves to thee! [5]
                                —J. EDGAR PARK

POEM:

Jesus shut within a book
Is hardly worth a passing look;
Jesus prisoned in a creed
Is a fruitless Lord, indeed.
But Jesus in the hearts of men
Shows His tenderness again.[6]
            —AUTHOR UNKNOWN

POEM:

The Jesus born of Mary
    When thirty years had flown

WE WOULD SEE JESUS

Was a carpenter of Judah,
Not otherwise was known.

The Jesus born of Spirit
Upon the Jordan's brink
In three years shook a nation
And made the ages think.

The Jesus born of Mary
Was crucified they say;
The Jesus born of Spirit
Still lives and builds today.[7]
—CHAUNCEY R. PIETY

PRAYER:

Our Father, help us to understand the meaning of the life of Jesus. From his teachings and the way he lived may we decide on our values and find his will for our lives. Help us to picture Jesus in situations like we face and from his example know how to choose what is right. When the road ahead seems hard, may we not choose the easy way but see our goal clearly and strive to reach it. Let our thoughts of Jesus bring us new vision, new hopes, and new desires. Make us steadfast and loyal and may we find our place in thy kingdom. In his name we pray. AMEN.

HYMN: "Rise Up, O Men of God" or
      "O Jesus, I Have Promised"

BENEDICTION:

May the love of God and the communion of the Holy Spirit abide with us all. AMEN.

SERVICE 12

THE POTENTIAL IN EACH OF US

PRELUDE: "Melody in F" (Rubinstein)

CALL TO WORSHIP:

> Lift up your heads, ye mighty gates,
> Behold, the King of Glory waits;
> The King of kings is drawing near;
> The Saviour of the world is here!
>
> Fling wide the portals of your heart;
> Make it a temple, set apart
> From earthly use for Heaven's employ,
> Adorned with prayer, and love, and joy.
>
> Redeemer, come, we open wide
> Our hearts to thee; here, Lord, abide.
> Thine inner presence let us feel;
> Thy grace and love in us reveal.
> —GEORGE WEISSEL
> TR. CATHERINE WINKWORTH

HYMN: "Take Thou Our Minds" or
"O Jesus, Thou Art Standing"

SCRIPTURE:

I am the vine, and my Father is the husbandman. Every branch in me that beareth not fruit he taketh away: and every branch that beareth fruit, he purgeth it, that it may bring forth more fruit. Now ye are clean through the word which I have spoken unto you. Abide in me, and I in you. As the branch cannot bear fruit of itself, except it abide in the vine; no more can ye, except ye abide in me. I am the vine, ye are the branches: He that abideth in me, and I in him, the same bringeth forth much fruit: for without me ye can do nothing. If a man abide not in me, he is cast forth as a branch, and is withered; and men gather them, and cast them into the fire, and they are burned. If ye abide in me, and my words abide in you, ye shall ask what ye will, and it shall be done unto you. Herein is my Father glorified, that ye bear much fruit; so shall ye be my disciples. As the Father hath loved me, so have I loved you: continue ye in my love. If ye keep my commandments, ye shall abide in my love; even as I have kept my Father's commandments, and abide in his love. These things have I spoken unto you, that my joy might remain in you, and that your joy might be full. This is my commandment, That ye love one another, as I have loved you. Greater love hath no man than this, that a man lay down his life for his friends. Ye are my friends, if ye do whatsoever I command you.[1]

STORY:

THE VISION OF ZACCHAEUS

When Jesus and his disciples reached Jericho, a great crowd gathered around them. There was a man named Zacchaeus who had heard about the teacher from Nazareth. Some had said that he was a prophet, others that he was the Messiah. Zacchaeus was determined to see him as he passed through the city.

Zacchaeus was a tax collector, and the people hated tax collectors. They were thought to be dishonest, but if not, they collected taxes for rulers like Herod, and that alone made the people resent them. The Jewish people disliked anyone who co-operated with the Roman government. Such a person would be a traitor to his own people. The Jews had to show respect socially to a tax collector, but they would never give him their friendship.

Zacchaeus probably worried about the fact that he had no friends among his own people. His importance as a tax collector and the wealth that he had piled up did not bring him the joy that he had expected. He had sufficient money to get everything he wanted except friendship. As he thought about it, he realized that the poorest beggar had more friends than he.

Zacchaeus was short of stature and could not see over the heads of the people in the crowd. He knew that no one was friendly enough to him to move a little and give him a chance to see. But he was determined to see Jesus anyway. He ran ahead of the crowd and climbed into a sycamore tree, so he could look down upon Jesus as he passed. Neither of these acts was in keeping with his dignity as a tax collector, but they showed his eagerness to carry out his purpose.

When Jesus passed by, he looked up and saw Zacchaeus. The words that he spoke brought great joy to the little man. At last someone had shown him friendliness. There was someone who did not resent him. He was very much surprised that that someone was an important teacher. The people were surprised also when Jesus stopped under the tree, looked up, and said, "Zacchaeus, make haste and come down. This day I must abide at your house."

The people standing nearby exchanged glances and whisperings that were full of meaning. The people began to murmur, saying that Jesus had gone to be the guest of a man who was a sinner.

Zacchaeus had been dissatisfied with his way of life for some time. He was tired of being on the edge of things, of having no friends. He wanted to set his life in a different direction. When he climbed out of the sycamore tree to welcome his new friend, he made up his mind to be different.

Zacchaeus knew that Jesus would be likely to lose some followers that day because of his choice of a place to stop. Going to the home of a tax collector would make him more unpopular with a great many people. Jesus was also aware of this, but he may have decided that it was worth taking the risk, for Zacchaeus needed a friend.

On that day, as Zacchaeus and his guest sat at the table talking, it was evident that Zacchaeus was tired of his way of life. As he looked into Jesus' eyes, he saw a vision of the man he might have been—the man he could have become. His life was laid bare as they talked together. He saw his own life as Jesus would see it. And he could not make a halfway commitment; he had to go all the way. He was sorry for his past mistakes and offered, as far as possible, to right the wrongs he had done.

When Zacchaeus took the step forward to the new and better way of life that Jesus had opened up to him, he may have gone to the door and announced to the people on the outside his decision. He said, "Behold, Lord, half of my goods I give to the poor; and if I have defrauded anyone of anything, I restore it fourfold." Jesus made it clear to Zacchaeus that he was forgiven for his past mistakes when he said to him, "Today salvation has come to this house."

THE POTENTIAL IN EACH OF US

LEADER:

We will hear the story of Zacchaeus as Luke has given it.

SCRIPTURE:

And Jesus entered and passed through Jericho. And, behold, there was a man named Zacchaeus, which was the chief among the publicans, and he was rich. And he sought to see Jesus who he was; and could not for the press, because he was little of stature. And he ran before, and climbed up into a sycamore tree to see him: for he was to pass that way. And when Jesus came to the place, he looked up, and saw him, and said unto him, Zacchaeus, make haste, and come down; for to day I must abide at thy house. And he made haste, and came down, and received him joyfully. And when they saw it, they all murmured, saying, That he was gone to be guest with a man that is a sinner. And Zacchaeus stood, and said unto the Lord; Behold, Lord, the half of my goods I give to the poor; and if I have taken any thing from any man by false accusation, I restore him fourfold. And Jesus said unto him, This day is salvation come to this house.[2]

POEM:

> Set yourself upon a hill
>   And on God's presence wait;
> Let thoughts wander where they will;
>   Sit and meditate.
>
> The horizon spreads, and the world's enclosed
>   By earth and sand and sod;
> And man builds up, his work imposed
>   Upon the firmament of God.
>
> A wall, a tower, a mighty road
>   Traversed by car or train—
> These things shall end, in rust corrode,
>   God's earth shall yet remain.
>
> A river's spanned by a fragile strand,
>   A tribute to man's skill;
> And yet we see on every hand,
>   God's world is greater still
>
> The things of men are wondrous great;
>   Onward, upward he does plod;

But can we see, before too late:
We must build on and up with God! [3]
—ROBERT A. KNOWLES

HYMN: "Once to Every Man and Nation" or
"O Young and Fearless Prophet"

PRAYER:
Our Father, who hast given to all people a desire to know thee, help us to feel that we are always in thy presence and thou art ready to hear us when we come in the right manner. Take from our lives anything that keeps us from being instruments in thy hands. Forbid that we should spend our days doing trivial things and miss the chance of sharing our blessings. Help us to be friendly with the lonely, kind to all we meet along the way, and willing to share with the needy. Grant us grace to overcome selfishness and weaknesses of every kind that we may be better followers of thine. In Jesus' name we pray. AMEN.

HYMN: "Give of Your Best to the Master" or
"Take My Life, and Let It Be"

BENEDICTION:
Dismiss us with thy blessing and help us to live by thy purpose for us. AMEN.

SERVICE 13

FRIENDS OF ALL

PRELUDE: Hymn tune "Dix"

CALL TO WORSHIP:

> For the joy of human love,
>> Brother, sister, parent, child,
> Friends on earth, and friends above;
>> For all gentle thoughts and mild:
> Lord of all, to thee we raise
>> This our hymn of grateful praise.[1]
>> —FOLLIOTT S. PIERPOINT

HYMN: "Now Thank We All Our God" or
"We Gather Together"

SCRIPTURE:

This is my commandment, That ye love one another, as I have loved you. Greater love hath no man than this, that a man lay down his life for his friends. Ye are my friends, if ye do whatsoever I command you. Henceforth I call you not servants; for the servant knoweth not what his lord doeth: but I have called you friends; for all things that I have heard of my Father I have made known unto you.

A friend loveth at all times.[2]

FROM LITERATURE:

The only way to have a friend is to be one.—RALPH WALDO EMERSON.

It is only the great-hearted who can be true friends. The mean and cowardly never know what true friendship means.—CHARLES KINGS-LEY.

PRAYER:

Our Father, we thank thee for all that our friends have meant to us, for those who have been an inspiration and have helped us to reach higher goals. Guide us in our friendships that we may choose worthy friends. Help us never to be content with second best but always strive to reach the highest standards. We thank thee for all the friendly people we have met along the way. Forgive us for our mistakes and help us to try again when we have failed. In Jesus' name we pray. AMEN.

POEM:

It is my joy in life to find
    At every turning of the road,
The strong arm of a comrade kind
    To help me onward with my load.
And since I have no gold to give,
    And love alone must make amends,
My only prayer is, while I live,—
    God make me worthy of my friends!
                    —FRANK D. SHERMAN

LEADER:

In the story that you will hear we may see how Jesus made friends.

STORY:

JESUS AND THE WOMAN OF SAMARIA

Jesus and his disciples were traveling through Samaria. Most Jews would go miles out of the way rather than pass through Samaria, so great was their hatred of the Samaritans.

Jesus had stopped at a well for a drink of water, while the disciples had gone into the town to buy food. He had nothing with which to draw water. Jesus saw a Samaritan woman who had come to the well for water, and asked her for a drink. She knew that Jews and Samaritans were not on speaking terms. It had all started when the Jews had refused to let the Samaritans have any part in building the Temple at Jerusalem.

When the woman recognized Jesus as a Jew, she said, "How is it that you, a Jew, ask a drink of me, a woman of Samaria? For Jews have no dealings with Samaritans."

In spite of her sarcastic remark Jesus replied in a kind, friendly manner, saying, "If you knew the gift of God, and who it is that is saying to you, 'Give me a drink,' you would have asked him, and he would have given you living water."

The woman did not understand what Jesus meant by "living water." This was a riddle, but it was so interesting that she forgot to be sarcastic. She asked, "Sir, you have nothing to draw with, and the well is deep; where do you get that living water? Are you greater than our father Jacob, who gave us the well and who drank from it himself, and his sons, and his cattle?"

Jesus said to her, "Everyone who drinks of this water will thirst again, but whoever drinks of the water that I shall give him will never thirst; the water that I shall give him will become in him a spring of water welling up to eternal life."

The woman did not understand the riddle, but she asked for the living water. She believed that the stranger had something—a mysterious power—that he could give her. She said, "Sir, give me this water, that I may not thirst, nor come here to draw."

Jesus began to explain to her what he meant. He began talking about her personal life and what she needed to satisfy her restless spirit once and for all. It would be as wonderful as finding a drink of water that would satisfy her thirst forever. This was the answer to the riddle that she had not been able to understand.

When she finally realized that he could give her a power beyond herself, she asked for it, even though she did not understand it. At once she wanted to share the good news with all who would listen to her. She left her water jar and went into the village, saying, "Come, see a man who told me all that I ever did. Can this be the Christ?" [3]

LEADER:

From this story let us notice how Jesus made friends. Jesus brushed aside all difficulties in the way of being a friend to this woman. She was sarcastic, but he remained kind and friendly. She was interested only in material things—such as water to quench her thirst—but Jesus was talking about things of the spirit—a way of life, the right attitude toward God and man.

Jesus did not ask, "Will this help me in building the kingdom of God? Will my enemies criticize me for being friendly with this woman?" He did not wait for her to be friendly. Probably he may have asked, "Does this woman need a friend? Can I help her? Is it right to be friendly with her?"

Jesus had close friends among those he knew. He often went to the home of Mary, Martha, and Lazarus of Bethany when he was near there. Other close friends were Peter, James, and John, his disciples. We, too, may have close friends who are interested in the same things as we are.

Let us think of some people who need our friendship, who need encouragement. What should we ask ourselves? If we have been too busy, thinking only of ourselves, and forgotten to be friendly, let us resolve to be more friendly with persons of other countries, of other races, or those who are handicapped in any way.

POEM:

> I will follow the upward road today,
>   I will keep my face to the light.
> I will think high thoughts as I go my way,
>   I will do what I know is right.
> I will look for the flowers by the side of the road,
>   I will laugh and love and be strong,
> I will try to lighten another's load
>   This day as I fare along.[4]

—MARY S. EDGAR

PRAYER:

Our Father, we thank thee for each friend that we have. Help us to find ways of being friendly toward everyone, especially persons who need a friend. Help us to understand the people who seem strange and different to us. Forgive us for the times when we did not allow others to be friendly with us. Help us to realize that giving and sharing of ourselves with others is Christ's way of life. In Jesus' name we pray. AMEN.

HYMN: "I Would Be True" or
"How Beauteous Were the Marks Divine"

BENEDICTION:

The Lord watch between me and thee while we are absent one from the other. AMEN.

SERVICE 14

FELLOW WORKMEN WITH GOD

PRELUDE: Hymn tune "Ein' Feste Burg"

CALL TO WORSHIP:
>Dream not of noble service elsewhere wrought;
>   The simple duty that awaits thy hand
>   Is God's voice uttering a divine command,
>Life's common deeds build all that saints have thought.[1]
>   —MINOT J. SAVAGE

HYMN: "Fight the Good Fight" or
    "A Mighty Fortress Is Our God"

PRAYER:
O Master of our lives, who courageously lived among friend and enemy alike and who did not resist when the soldiers took thee by force, help us to learn how to resist evil, to overcome evil with good, and to live by thy plan for us. Fill us with thy spirit and make plain the way we should go. In thy name we pray. AMEN.

RESPONSIVE READING:
Leader: Fight the good fight of faith.
Group: Go, labor on! spend and be spent;
            Thy joy to do the Father's will:
        It is the way the Master went—
            Should not the servant tread it still?
Leader: Wait on the Lord: be of good courage, and he shall strengthen thine heart.

Group: Go, labor on! 'tis not for nought,
    Thine earthly loss is heav'nly gain;
    Men heed thee, love thee, praise thee not;
    The Master praises—what are men?

Leader: Be strong and of a good courage, fear not, nor be afraid of
    them: for the Lord thy God, he it is that doth go with thee;
    he will not fail thee, nor forsake thee.[2]

Group: Go, labor on! while it is day;
    The world's dark night is hastening on:
    Speed, speed thy work, cast sloth away;
    It is not thus that souls are won.

                    —Horatius Bonar

Story:

HE DARED TO BE BRAVE

Daniel was a member of the little kingdom of Judah. When he was a young man, the king of Babylon waged war on Judah and carried away many of the Jews as captives. Daniel, one of the captives, had been taught in the wisdom of his people. He believed in God and obeyed all of his commandments. From his childhood he had been wiser and more skillful than most of the other boys.

The Jewish people had many customs that were natural to them but that would seem strange to us today. They had rules about food, cleanliness, prayer, and every phase of life. There were many kinds of food they were allowed to eat and others that were forbidden. These rules were studied and observed carefully. Having been trained in these customs, Daniel tried to keep all of the rules.

The king of Babylon ordered that some of the finest young men who had been captured in the wars be brought to his palace. They would live at the court with the other princes, be taught the language of the people, and fed at the king's table. In this way they would be prepared for important work in the kingdom. The king became interested in Daniel and three of his friends who were among those selected.

Life would be easier for the Jewish boys at the king's palace. However, if they ate the rich food at the king's table, they would violate the rules of their religion and endanger their health. They had a difficult decision to make.

The king's servant urged them to eat the king's food. He was afraid that if they failed to do this, they would become pale and thin, and the king would blame him. Daniel, believing that he must be true to his religious training, said to the servant, "Let us eat our own food for ten days, and let the Babylonian boys eat the king's food for the same time. After that let us come together and see what has happened." Daniel was sure that the king would be pleased with the results.

The servant did as Daniel suggested, and after ten days the Jewish boys and the Babylonian boys were brought in. It was plain to everyone that Daniel and his friends were stronger and healthier than those who had eaten at the king's table. Afterward the Jewish boys were allowed to eat the plain, simple food that they had been brought up to eat.

Later the king was troubled because of a dream. He ordered that the wise men of the kingdom be brought together to interpret the dream. When they were brought in, the king had forgotten his dream. He wanted the wise men to tell him not only his dream but also the meaning of it. When they were unable to do this, the king became angry and threatened to have all of them put to death.

In this dilemma the king's servant thought of Daniel and suggested that he would be able to tell the king his dream and interpret it. When the young man was brought before the king, he explained that the dream was a prophecy of things to come. The king was satisfied and ordered that Daniel and his three friends be given positions of honor in the kingdom.

Daniel took a great risk when he decided to go against the orders of the king, but he could not do otherwise and be true to his religion. His decision was right when he "purposed in his heart that he would not defile himself with the portion of the king's meat, nor with the wine which he drank." He had the courage to do right even when he might have to suffer for it.

LEADER:

The hymn "Faith for Our Times" is a new hymn written by Barbara Owen for use during National Youth Week. Miss Owen is a minister of music of the Congregational Church.

HYMN:

>Faith for our times, O Lord, we pray,
>Clear guiding faith for life today;
>Thy wisdom and true insight give;
>Grant us a faith by which to live.

Faith in Thy Son, O Lord, we ask;
Faith to accept his every task.
Childlike we put our trust in thee;
Loose us from doubt and set us free.

We lacking faith are weak and frail;
But with its strength we shall prevail,
Valiant to mount each rugged height
Girded by trust in God's own might.[3]
—BARBARA J. OWEN

POEM:

I live to hail the season,
    By gifted ones foretold,
When man shall live by reason,
    And not alone by gold;
When man to man united,
And every wrong thing righted,
The whole world shall be lighted,
    As Eden was of old.

I live for those who love me,
    For those who know me true;
For the heaven that smiles above me,
    And awaits my spirit too;
For the cause that lacks assistance,
For the wrong that needs resistance,
For the future in the distance,
    And the good that I can do.[4]
—G. LINNAEUS BANKS

PRAYER:

Our Father, we are grateful for the record of the lives of the courageous men of the past who lived close to thee and who endured the hard things of life. We thank thee for those who did not count their lives of greatest importance but were more concerned with right living. Help us to learn from their example how always to be on the side of right and to be courageous in spite of opposition. Grant us strength to follow our convictions and to be true to the heritage that has been passed on to us. In the name of the Master of us all we pray. AMEN.

HYMN: "Dare to Be Drave" or
"I Would Be True"

BENEDICTION:
Now may thy spirit guide and direct us and keep us faithful follow-ers of thine. AMEN.

SERVICE 15

HOW SHALL
WE CHOOSE OUR WORK?

PRELUDE: Hymn tune "Laudes Domini"

CALL TO WORSHIP:
> O teach me, Lord, that I may teach
> The precious things thou dost impart;
> And wing my words, that they may reach
> The hidden depths of many a heart.
> —FRANCES R. HAVERGAL

HYMN: "My Master Was a Worker" or
"We Thank Thee, Lord, Thy Paths of Service Lead"

SCRIPTURE:
Jesus called them unto him, and said, Ye know that the princes of the Gentiles exercise dominion over them, and they that are great exercise authority upon them. But it shall not be so among you: but whoever will be great among you, let him be your minister; . . . even as the Son of man came not to be ministered unto, but to minister, and to give his life a ransom for many. . . . No man can serve two masters: for either he will hate the one, and love the other; or else he will hold to the one, and despise the other. Ye cannot serve God and mammon.[1]

POEM:
> From thee all skill and science flow,
> All pity, care, and love,

94

HOW SHALL WE CHOOSE OUR WORK?

All calm and courage, faith and hope;
O pour them from above.

And part them, Lord, to each and all,
As each and all shall need,
To rise like incense, each to thee,
In noble thought and deed.

And hasten, Lord, that perfect day,
When pain and death shall cease,
And thy just rule shall fill the earth
With health, and light, and peace.

When ever blue the sky shall gleam,
And ever green the sod,
And man's rude work deface no more
The Paradise of God.

—CHARLES KINGSLEY

LEADER:

We will hear the story of Florence Nightingale, who felt a call to be a nurse and raised nursing to a place of honor.

STORY:

FLORENCE NIGHTINGALE

Florence Nightingale grew up in a home of wealth and received a good education. Her father, wanting her to be a scholar, taught her Latin and Greek. Her mother, a society leader, insisted on taking her to parties. Florence wanted to do something worth while but was not sure what work to do. However, she often missed parties in order to nurse a sick child of a neighbor.

At twenty years of age Florence met Elizabeth Fry, a Quaker who had founded an order for nurses. Much impressed with Mrs. Fry's work, she began visiting hospitals at every opportunity. She was shocked at the noise, dirt, and lack of system in English hospitals. Sensing the great need for better care of the sick, she had a great desire to improve conditions in hospitals.

Florence heard of Kaiserwerth, a Protestant hospital on the Rhine in Germany that was different. While traveling in Europe, she stopped there and found a clean, well-organized hospital with decent nurses. She left her traveling party and stayed there a few months to study nursing. Her parents were horrified that their daughter should join working women and do menial labor like nursing. Nevertheless, she was convinced that she must learn how to operate a hospital by learning all she could as a nurse. Florence advanced quickly, for she showed great eagerness in her work.

Upon her return to England, Florence announced to her parents that she felt a call to nurse the sick and improve conditions in hospitals. They protested and for some time kept her from taking any more steps toward her goal. However, she wrote in her diary: "I am thirty years old, the age at which Christ began his mission. Now no more childish things—no more vain things. Lord, let me think only of thy will."

Secretly the young lady studied everything she could obtain on nursing and soon knew more about the subject than anyone else in England. When she learned that a small hospital for women teachers needed a superintendent, she applied and got the position. Her parents felt that the work would ruin her health. It was a difficult task, for in addition to operating the Harley Street Hospital, she had to raise money to supplement its income. In a short while she had the hospital well organized and many improvements made in nursing. She was happy now for she was doing what she wanted most of all to do.

In the autumn of 1854 England and France were thrown into war with Russia. The British were unprepared and could send only a few doctors, nurses, and medical supplies. Miss Nightingale read of the high death rate of wounded men in the hospital that had been set up in Scutari across the straits from Constantinople. She was ready to volunteer when the Secretary of War asked her to organize a force of nurses and serve in that area. This was a big undertaking, but her training at Kaiserwerth and in London were preparation for this new assignment.

Miss Nightingale and twenty nurses sailed for Scutari in the Black Sea north of Turkey. They were amazed at what they saw—along the five miles of cots and beds set up in the corridors there were the discouraged, sick, and wounded men. The doctors resented the coming of the women nurses and were not co-operative, but when the results of good nursing appeared, they felt differently.

The determined young lady with the aid of her nurses set out to bring order out of chaos. She outfitted a kitchen and began serving suitable meals to the sick. She started a crew of two hundred convalescent soldiers scrubbing floors and improving sanitation. She enlisted the wives of the soldiers to do the laundry. She and her helpers worked twenty hours a day ministering to the sick and improving conditions. When the death rate dropped from 60 per cent to 1 per cent, the doctors showed more consideration to the nurses.

At night Miss Nightingale would walk along the rows of beds with a lamp in her hand giving encouragement to the soldiers. They looked forward to the daily visit of the "Lady with the Lamp" as they called her. Later after many of them returned to the battlefields, she rode among them and received an ovation. She organized classes for convalescent soldiers, for everyone, rich or poor, was important to her as a person. The men loved and honored her because she had made it possible for them to survive their wounds and illness, and to continue fighting for their country.

Miss Nightingale visited three other hospitals in Crimea and helped to make them into well-regulated institutions for the sick. Afterward she contracted a fever from which she barely recovered. The doctors urged her to return to England for rest, but she felt that if the soldiers could endure suffering, so could she. When the fever passed, she was left an invalid for years. During this time she wrote letters and received many visitors in an effort to improve conditions in hospitals.

The British people were so grateful for her service that they donated $250,000 which she used to set up a training school for nurses. To the end of Florence Nightingale's life there were many celebrations honoring the "Lady with the Lamp," and large sums of money were raised for hospital reforms.

POEM:

Father, whose will is life and good
  For all of mortal breath
Bind strong the bond of brotherhood
  Of those who fight with death.

Empower the hands and hearts and wills
  Of friends in lands afar,
Who battle with the body's ills,
  And wage thy holy war.

Where'er they heal the maimed and blind,
  Let love of Christ attend;

Proclaim the good Physician's mind,
And prove the Saviour friend.

For still his love works wondrous charms,
And, as in days of old,
He takes the wounded to his arms,
And bears them to the fold.
—HARDWICKE D. RAWNSLEY

PRAYER:

Our Father, may we realize that we are always in thy presence and that thou art ready to guide us in our choices. Help us to live close to thee that we shall receive impressions coming from thee. Reveal thy plan for our lives and open up ways of preparing ourselves to serve thee. We thank thee for those like Florence Nightingale who have pioneered in nursing and made the way easier for us. Show us our work, guide us step by step, and help us to begin now preparing ourselves to be an instrument in thy hands, in the name of Christ who said, "I am come that they might have life, and that they might have it more abundantly," we pray. AMEN.

HYMN: "Hark, the Voice of Jesus Calling" or
"Dear Master, in Whose Life I See" or
"Fairest Lord Jesus"

BENEDICTION:

May the blessing of God abide with you and his spirit guide you, now and evermore. AMEN.

SERVICE 16

FAITH GIVES COURAGE

PRELUDE: Music to hymn tune "Germany"

CALL TO WORSHIP:

> Strong Son of God, immortal Love,
>> Whom we, that have not seen thy face,
>> By faith, and faith alone, embrace,
> Believing where we cannot prove;

> . . . .

> Thou seemest human and divine,
>> The highest, holiest manhood, thou.
>> Our wills are ours, we know not how;
> Our wills are ours, to make them thine.

> Our little systems have their day;
>> They have their day and cease to be;
>> They are but broken lights of thee,
> And thou, O Lord, art more than they.

> We have but faith: we cannot know,
>> For knowledge is of things we see;
>> And yet we trust it comes from thee,
> A beam in darkness: let it grow.[1]
>> —ALFRED TENNYSON

HYMN: "Thou Art the Way" or
    "My Faith Looks Up to Thee"

SCRIPTURE:

Now faith is the substance of things hoped for, the evidence of things not seen. For by it the elders obtained a good report. Through faith we understand that the worlds were framed by the word of God, so that things which are seen were not made of things which do appear. By faith Abel offered unto God a more excellent sacrifice than Cain, by which he obtained witness that he was righteous, God testifying of his gifts: and by it he being dead yet speaketh. By faith Enoch was translated that he should not see death; and was not found, because God had translated him: for before his translation he had this testimony, that he pleased God. But without faith it is impossible to please him: for he that cometh to God must believe that he is, and that he is a rewarder of them that diligently seek him. . . . By faith Abraham, when he was called to go out into a place which he should after receive for an inheritance, obeyed; and he went out, not knowing whither he went. By faith he sojourned in the land of promise, as in a strange country, dwelling in tabernacles with Isaac and Jacob, the heirs with him of the same promise: for he looked for a city which hath foundations, whose builder and maker is God. . . . These all died in faith, not having received the promises, but having seen them afar off. . . . But now they desire a better country, that is, an heavenly: wherefore God is not ashamed to be called their God: for he hath prepared for them a city.[2]

POEM:

> Build on, and make thy castles high and fair,
>   Rising and reaching upward to the skies;
> Listen to voices in the upper air,
>   Nor lose thy simple faith in mysteries.[3]
>   —HENRY W. LONGFELLOW

POEM:

> The wise may bring their learning,
>   The rich may bring their wealth,
> And some may bring their greatness,
>   And some bring strength and health;
> We, too, would bring our treasures
>   To offer to the King.
>
> . . . .
>
> We'll bring him hearts that love him;
>   We'll bring him thankful praise,

FAITH GIVES COURAGE

The young souls meekly striving
To walk in holy ways:
And these shall be the treasures
We offer to the King.[4]

—Author unknown

Story:

A MAIDEN'S FAITH

A marauding band of Syrian soldiers swooped down on Israel and carried away many captives. Among them was a little Jewish girl whose name we do not know. By this act she was robbed of her home, parents, and freedom. When the general, Naaman, returned with the captives, he gave the little girl to his wife as a maid. She was attractive and intelligent, or she would not have been given the privilege of living in the general's home.

Naaman was a great man with his master, the king. He was in high favor because of the victory he had won over Israel. He was honored in his country and moved in the highest social circles. But there was tragedy in his home, for he had an incurable disease. He was a leper. It is surprising that he kept up his work and lived as normally as he did.

It seems that the little maid bore no resentment toward Naaman because of her fate. She had every reason to hate the man who was responsible for her capture. He had robbed her of her freedom, but he could not take away her faith in her God and her desire to help. All of her actions showed love and good will toward her captor.

The little girl suffered with the general and his wife because of his leprosy, but she was not sure that she would be permitted to help. At last she decided to speak regardless of whether the general liked it or not. One day she timidly remarked to her mistress, "I wish that my lord were with the prophet that is in Samaria, for he would cure him of his leprosy." She had faith, for she had grown up in the same section with the prophet Elisha and knew of the wonders that he had performed.

Naturally the general's wife was interested in anything that might restore her husband's health. She was eager to know if the prophet could really cure leprosy. The little maid had faith that if given the opportunity, the prophet would call upon God and the general would be healed. Her words were repeated to the king, and he joined with the wife in urging Naaman to go to see the prophet in Samaria.

101

The king whose armies had conquered that of the king of Israel sent a valuable present and a letter to the king of Israel. He demanded that the king, not the prophet, should cure Naaman. That showed that he had not listened carefully to the words of the little maid.

When the king of Israel read the letter, he was frightened. He said, "Am I God, to kill or to make alive, that this man sends word to me to cure a man of his leprosy? Is he seeking a quarrel with me?" When Elisha heard of this, he suggested that the king send the general to him, then he would know that there was a prophet in Israel.

So the little maiden watched as her master set out on the visit to the prophet of whom she had told him. There may have been doubts in Naaman's mind that he would be cured, but there was none in the mind of the maid.

When Naaman reached the home of the prophet, for some reason Elisha did not even go out to see him. He sent a servant to tell him to go and dip seven times in the Jordan River. The great man was angry and went away, saying, "I thought that he would surely come out to me, and stand, and call on the name of the Lord his God."

A general who gives commands is not likely to follow an order given by a prophet who is not courteous enough to come out to speak to him. He said, "Are there not rivers in Damascus better than all the rivers of Israel? Could I not wash in them, and be clean?"

A servant of Naaman suggested, "My lord, if the prophet had commanded you to do some great thing, would you not have done it? How much rather, then, when he said to you, 'Wash and be clean'? The command from the prophet was so simple that even the least could have done it."

Naaman saw the wisdom of the words of the servant, and he went and dipped himself seven times in the Jordan, and his flesh was restored like the flesh of a little child, and he was clean.

In Naaman's house there was great rejoicing because the master was healed. And it all came about because the little maid had faith in God and good will toward her master.

PoEM:

> When the anchors that faith has cast
>   Are dragging in the gale,
> I am quietly holding fast
>   To the things that cannot fail:

FAITH GIVES COURAGE

I know that right is right;
That it is not good to lie;
That love is better than spite,
And a neighbor than a spy;

I know that passion needs
The leash of a sober mind;
I know that generous deeds
Some sure reward will find;

In the darkest night of the year,
When the stars have all gone out,
That courage is better than fear,
That faith is truer than doubt.[5]
—WASHINGTON GLADDEN

LEADER:
We will sing the hymn "Lord, We Believe," a new hymn written by Thomas Paul Slavens for use during National Youth Week. The author is a pastor of the Christian Church.

HYMN:
Lord, we believe; help thou our unbelief;
Show us the way.
Till thee we seek, we cannot find relief
Or fears allay.
Where now we grope for faith to meet our needs,
Help us to find the way the true path leads.

Lord, we believe; O speak to us today
In accents clear.
Throw thy bright beams of love across our way;
Cast out our fear.
Grant us the faith in God which Christ revealed
That unbelief to sure belief may yield.

Lord, we believe; help us our faith to live
And stedfast be.
Thou hast so loved, help us our love to give
With joy to thee.

Let doubt give way and faith our spirits fill
With power to know and do thy holy will.[6]

—THOMAS PAUL SLAVENS

PRAYER:

O God, who art the strength of our lives, increase our faith for we know that without faith it is impossible to please thee. Grant us faith that will dispel fear, and hope that will banish doubt. Help us to put our entire trust in thee at all times. May every experience of our lives be a means of growth in Christian character. Help us to believe that beauty, goodness, and truth will always abide. Lead us into abundant life. We pray in the name of him who said, "I have overcome the world." AMEN.

HYMN: "Faith of Our Fathers!" or
"Dear Lord and Father of Mankind"

BENEDICTION:

Dismiss us with thy blessing and grant us strength and courage in the days that are ahead. AMEN.

SERVICE 17

BUILDING IN GOD'S PLAN

PRELUDE: "The Lark's Song" by Tschaikowsky

CALL TO WORSHIP:
I will meditate in thy precepts, and have respect unto thy ways.
I will delight myself in thy statutes: I will not forget thy word.[1]

HYMN: "Rejoice, Ye Pure in Heart" or
"Joyful, Joyful, We Adore Thee"

POEM:
We would be building; temples still undone
O'er crumbling walls their crosses scarcely lift
Waiting till love can raise the broken stone,
And hearts creative bridge the human rift;
We would be building, Master, let thy plan
Reveal the life that God would give to man.

Teach us to build; upon the solid rock
We set the dream that hardens into deed,
Ribbed with the steel that time and change doth mock,
Th' unfailing purpose of our noblest creed;
Teach us to build; O Master, lend us sight
To see the towers gleaming in the light.

O keep us building, Master; may our hands
Ne'er falter when the dream is in our hearts,
When to our ears there come divine commands

And all the pride of sinful will departs;
We build with thee, O grant enduring worth
Until the heav'nly Kingdom comes on earth.[2]
—PURD E. DEITZ

SCRIPTURE:

We are fellow workmen for God; you are God's field, God's building. According to the commission of God given to me, like a skilled master-builder I laid a foundation, and another man is building upon it. Let each man take care how he builds upon it. For no other foundation can any one lay than that which is laid, which is Jesus Christ. Now if any one builds on the foundation with gold, silver, precious stones, wood, hay, stubble—each man's work will become manifest; for the Day will disclose it, because it will be revealed with fire, and the fire will test what sort of work each one has done. If the work which any man has built on the foundation survives, he will receive a reward. If any man's work is burned up, he will suffer loss, though he himself will be saved, but only as through fire. Do you not know that you are God's temple and that God's Spirit dwells in you? If any one destroys God's temple, God will destroy him. For God's temple is holy, and that temple you are.[3]

LEADER:

We will hear a story of Nehemiah, the builder.

STORY:

NEHEMIAH THE BUILDER

Nehemiah was the son of Jewish captives but was liked and trusted at the Persian court. The king had made him his cupbearer.

From his mother the young man had learned about Jerusalem, the sacred city of the Jewish people. She had described the Temple where the people worship. The Temple more than anything else helped them to know God.

Nehemiah talked with travelers from Jerusalem who told him that the once beautiful city was in ruins; the walls were down and the gates were burned. The young man was distressed over the news.

Once when Nehemiah came into the king's presence to bring him wine, one glance showed that something was wrong. The king inquired, "Are you ill?" The young man replied, "No, I am not sick. I am sad because Jerusalem, the city that my forefathers loved, is in ruins." The king wanted to know what he was expected to do.

Nehemiah hesitated while he asked God to show him what to say. He replied, "If I have won the king's favor, would the king allow me to go back to help build the city again?" The king wanted to know how long it would take and if Nehemiah would come back again. He answered as well as he could, and the king gave him permission to go.

The young man could have gone on living very pleasantly in Babylon, but he wanted to help his people restore the sacred city that meant so much to them. He knew that it would be difficult, and he prayed that God would give him strength to do it.

The king gave him letters to the Persian governors of the countries through which he would pass. He also gave an order to the officer in charge of the king's forests, asking him to give Nehemiah timber to rebuild the walls and the gates of the holy city.

At last the young man began his journey with a glad heart and with great hopes. When he reached Jerusalem, conditions were worse than he had expected. On a tour of inspection his horse could barely get through the streets on account of the piles of rubbish.

On the next day he called the chief men of the city together, saying, "God has sent me here to do this work, and he will help us with it. He has also touched the heart of the king of Persia, who has given us an order to use lumber from his own forests. This is a difficult task, but we can do it. Come now, let us rise up and build."

With encouragement from a leader they could trust and follow, the men began the work of rebuilding the walls. Nehemiah divided up the task, giving to each man a special part of the wall to build. The work did not seem so great as before, for everyone did his part faithfully. The men had a mind to work.

There were enemies on the outside who did not like the Jewish people and tried in many ways to stop the work. Men had to be appointed to guard the workers; others with trumpets warned when danger threatened. Nehemiah was on guard most of the time.

In spite of the enemies the work was finished; the walls were rebuilt, and the gates were put in place. It had been difficult, but by working together and helping one another, the people could now live in peace while the rest of the city was rebuilt.

A great celebration was planned. Ezra, the scribe, was asked to copy on papyrus the history of the Jewish people and the laws that God had given them. When they came together, the scribe read the things God had done for the people and also the laws that he expected them to follow.

When this was finished, Nehemiah went back to Babylon as he had promised the king. He reported to the king all that he had done. Later when allowed to return to Jerusalem, he saw things that displeased him. The people had not kept the laws as he had hoped they would. He urged them to call upon God for help and be more faithful in observing all of the laws and customs.

Nehemiah was grateful that the king had given him permission to go to Jerusalem and had helped with the work. He was also thankful that God had given him strength for the task. He was pleased that the people had a mind to work, for the building could not have been done unless all had worked together.

POEM:

> O God, I want to build with thee,
>   With hands and mind create.
> Help me a greater vision see
>   As on thy will I wait.
>
> Help me to build a better world,
>   Where peace and love may dwell
> With flags of brotherhood unfurled,
>   And songs of joy do swell.
>
> But first, O God, help me to find
>   My own life in thy plan.
> Let selfish thoughts be put behind,
>   In love for fellow man.
>
> Let me build my own life strong
>   On Christ the cornerstone;
> Thy praise shall be my daily song,
>   My will thy very own.[4]
>   —ROBERT A. KNOWLES

PRAYER:

Our Father, we thank thee for a new day, for all new beginnings. Forgive us if we have been too busy with our own affairs to discover ways of serving thee. May we seek first the kingdom of God, seize every opportunity to help bring thy kingdom on earth, and strive to make the world a better place to live. Give us faith that evil will be overcome with good. Help us to build into our lives the qualities that will endure—truth, purity, honesty, loyalty, and meekness; through Jesus Christ we pray. AMEN.

HYMN: "Give of Your Best to the Master" or
      "Truehearted, Wholehearted, Faithful and Loyal"

BENEDICTION:
   The Lord watch over us, and may we serve thee better and hasten the coming of thy kingdom. AMEN.

SERVICE 18

GROWING IN GOD'S PLAN

PRELUDE: Hymn tune "Sheltered Dale"

CALL TO WORSHIP:
O come, let us worship and bow down:
Let us kneel before the Lord our maker.
For he is our God;
And we are the people of his pasture, and the sheep of his hand.[1]

HYMN: "Open My Eyes" or
"Draw Thou My Soul"

SCRIPTURE:
Blessed is the man that walketh not in the counsel of the ungodly, nor standeth in the way of sinners, nor sitteth in the seat of the scornful.

But his delight is in the law of the Lord; and in his law doth he meditate day and night.

And he shall be like a tree planted by the rivers of water, that bringeth forth his fruit in his season; his leaf also shall not wither; and whatsoever he doeth shall prosper.

The ungodly are not so: but are like the chaff which the wind driveth away.

Therefore the ungodly shall not stand in the judgment, nor sinners in the congregation of the righteous.

For the Lord knoweth the way of the righteous: but the way of the ungodly shall perish.[2]

GROWING IN GOD'S PLAN

PRAYER:

O Master of our lives, we would have a closer fellowship with thee. Help us as we meditate quietly to open our minds to guidance that we receive from thee. Grant that our religious customs may go deeper than a habit and become the giving of ourselves to thy cause. Lead us into better ways of serving thee as we strive to follow thee. In thy name we pray. AMEN.

LEADER:

As we hear the story of the "Little Acorn," let us think of ways that we may grow.

STORY:

THE LITTLE ACORN

Once there was a beautiful acorn that grew on the topmost twig of a large oak tree. From a tiny speck of green in the spring it grew, until in the fall it became a large, beautiful brown acorn with a lustrous, shiny shell.

Being the highest acorn on the mother tree, it was the first to see the sun rise in the morning and the last to see it set at night. In fact, it saw a great deal because of its exalted position. Birds perched there, on the highest limb, to escape boys' slingshots. These birds brought endless news and chatter.

The mockingbird, with its rich repertoire of songs, gave the acorn a wonderful knowledge of music. Migratory birds, going South for the winter, brought news of arctic snows and tropic heat and places far away.

The crows, wisest of all birds, cawed away in the high branches, giving forth words of wisdom, passed on by generations of ancestors. The acorn never ceased to be amazed at their knowledge.

Indeed, this little acorn was the smartest, best-educated, and proudest acorn on the whole tree, and there were thousands of them. It looked down on its brothers and sisters, that is, when it gave them any thought at all.

One chilly fall day something terrible happened. The winds blew and rains fell. Hundreds of acorns fell to the ground. Our topmost acorn was terribly alarmed. It had presumed that life would go on forever, each day better than the previous one. Truly frightened, it asked the mother tree: "Mother, must I fall too?"

"Yes, my child," mother tree whispered gently, "all acorns must fall to the ground. When I was an acorn, I fell, too, though you might not think so by looking at my strong branches now. You might be wise to let go and fall now instead of waiting to be blown off and land poorly. But, that's up to you."

The ground was so far down. So many big limbs were in between. Besides, who wanted to abandon such a perfect position, especially when the birds were flying South, full of the latest news up North.

It clung closely to the twig. Several hard rains came. Its hold became weaker and weaker. One day mother tree said: "You had better go now, my child, and may God bless you."

The little acorn looked down. How far the ground looked! And what dangers lurked there? It grew dizzy and faint from just looking.

It closed its eyes, said a prayer, and let go. Z-z-z-z-z-z—the air whistled past. Then, "clickle"; it landed softly on brown leaves below.

Life below was no bed of roses. Cows trampled the ground, crushing many acorns with their hard, heavy hoofs. Pigs came and ate literally thousands, cruelly crunching their beautiful shells and eating the sweet meat inside. Squirrels picked up hundreds of others, bearing them off to some dreadful hiding place.

Our little acorn, frightened as it was, kept very still. It managed to roll under a leaf and escape detection.

Finally, snow covered the ground, and all dangers ceased. The acorn fell into a long, drowsy sleep.

Spring came. The snow melted. The sun rose higher. The acorn awoke. Poor thing, its once lovely shell was now dull and ugly. But it was alive.

Then its head began to ache terribly. What an ache!

"Help, Mother! I'm sick!" it cried.

"My child, you're not sick at all. You're perfectly well. Your headache means you're sprouting. I remember how my head hurt when I sprouted."

Now sprouting is what every acorn is meant for, if they're lucky enough to escape the cows' hoofs, the pigs' teeth, and the squirrels' hiding places. When an acorn sprouts, its shell splits, and the seed within sends a root downward and a two-leafed twig upward. Mother tree explained all this.

"But that means I will die. There will be no more me. I don't want to change. I want to stay like I am. The world is terribly unfair!"

"Yes, my child, I felt once as you do. But look around the ground, and you'll see some of your older brothers and sisters who refused to sprout last year. Do you want to become like them?"

All around were dirty, rotten shells of what had been acorns a year before. They were so decayed that not even a pig would take notice of them. As much as our little acorn dreaded sprouting, it feared *that* kind of fate worse.

"All right, Mother," it said, "I'll sprout if I must. And if I should become half as lovely and strong as you, I won't even mind the pain."

That night it rained, and the next day the acorn's shell split open. How it did hurt! Then, there came a wonderful and happy feeling to the little acorn.

Weeks and months passed. Fall came and found a strong little oak tree three inches high, strongly rooted in the ground.

Today, if you'll visit the spot, you will find two trees. One, the mother tree, is getting old. Before many years it will fall to the ground or be cut down by woodcutters.

Beside it is a straight, slender young oak. Birds perch in its high limbs. Some build their nests there. Others bring interesting news as they migrate North and South.

Because it dared fall to the ground, because it chose to give up its coat and cease being an acorn, because it was willing to grow, even though it hurt, our little acorn is now this lovely tree.[3]

Poem:
    All around us worlds are dying and new worlds are being born;
    All around us life is dying and life is being born.
    The fruit ripens on the tree;
    The roots are silently at work in the darkness of the earth
    Against a time when there shall be new leaves, fresh blossoms,
       green fruit.
    Such is the growing edge!
    It is the extra breath from the exhausted lung,
    The one more thing to try when all else has failed,
    The upward reach of life when weariness closes in upon all
       endeavor.
    This is the basis of hope in moments of despair,
    The incentive to carry on when times are out of joint
    And men have lost their reason; the source of confidence
    When worlds crash and dreams whiten into ash.
    The birth of a child—life's most dramatic answer to death—
    This is the growing edge incarnate.
      Look well to the growing edge![4]

—Howard Thurman

PRAYER:

Our Father, when we think of man, whom thou hast created, our minds are filled with wonder at thy greatness. When we think of the universe that thou hast made for man to use and enjoy, we are grateful to be alive in such a world. Help us to understand the laws that govern the universe and discover ways of living unselfish lives. Help us to grow as Jesus did in body, mind, and spirit, and in favor with God and man. Lift us to higher levels of Christian living and open up new ways of serving thee. We pray in the name of him who said he "came not to be ministered unto, but to minister." AMEN.

HYMN: "O Master, Let Me Walk with Thee" or
"O Jesus, I Have Promised"

BENEDICTION:

Now may the light that shone in Jesus Christ our Lord,
Shine in our hearts and mind by the indwelling Word;
And may the radiance which faith and hope restore,
Be and abide with us both now and evermore. AMEN.

—AUTHOR UNKNOWN

SERVICE 19

LIVING WITH YOUR SELF

PRELUDE: "Ode to Thanksgiving" by Beethoven

CALL TO WORSHIP:
> None but one can harm you,
> None but yourself who are your greatest foe;
> He that respects himself is safe from others:
> He wears a coat of mail that none can pierce.
> —HENRY W. LONGFELLOW

HYMN: "God of Our Youth, to Whom We Yield" or
"The Body, Lord, Is Ours to Keep"

SCRIPTURE:
Not that I have already obtained this or am already perfect; but I press on to make it my own, because Christ Jesus has made me his own. Brethren, I do not consider that I have made it my own; but one thing I do, forgetting what lies behind and straining forward to what lies ahead, I press on toward the goal for the prize of the upward call of God in Christ Jesus. . . .

Finally, brethren, whatever is true, whatever is honorable, whatever is just, whatever is pure, whatever is lovely, whatever is gracious, if there is any excellence, if there is anything worthy of praise, think about these things.[1]

FROM LITERATURE:
> This above all: to thine own self be true,
> And it must follow, as the night the day,
> Thou canst not then be false to any man.[2]
> —WILLIAM SHAKESPEARE

My strength is as the strength of ten,
Because my heart is pure.[3]
—ALFRED TENNYSON

For when the One Great Scorer comes
To write against your name,
He writes—not that you won or lost—
But how you played the game.[4]
—GRANTLAND RICE

LEADER:

As you listen to the story of the "Silver Peso," will you decide how you would have met the situation that Josef faced?

STORY:

THE SILVER PESO

As the sun disappeared over the low green hills and the chill of evening settled in the valley, Josef walked faster along the dusty road that led to San Gabriel Mission. In those early days, a hundred years ago in California, when there were few white men in the land, brave padres, or priests of the Catholic Church, had built these Missions in the wilderness. Here the padres taught the Indians about God and how to do useful things such as weaving cloth and raising wheat. Besides taking the place of churches, schools and workshops, the Missions served as free hotels to any travelers who might be journeying up or down the coast.

Josef, as he thought of the huge crackling fire of logs and the steaming hot supper a little way ahead, should have been cheerful and happy. He was young and strong, and was not tired with walking. The evening was clear and lovely. A mocking bird sang himself to sleep in a palm tree by the road. But Josef's face was gloomy. One hand thrust deep into his trousers pocket clutched his last peso, a silver coin worth about a dollar. The feel of it made him angry. It was all he had in the world except a little bundle of clothes under his arm.

That year Josef had had bad luck. He had owned a fine herd of cattle that spent the summer browsing on the short grass of the hills. He had gone into the mountains to look for gold and when he returned his cattle were lost, probably chased far away by wolves. Neither had he found the gold, though other men told him it lay buried in the rocks of the great mountains. Bitter and discouraged, he had started to walk south into Mexico, all his money spent except one silver peso.

As Josef walked along, a wicked idea was shaping itself in his mind. He knew that in the church of the Mission were four beautiful silver candlesticks brought all the way across the water from Spain. Slender candles were kept always burning in them. He said to himself, "I will steal a candlestick in the night and carry it under my coat down into Mexico, where I will sell it. Then I will have more money to put with my one peso."

Across the fields came the sound of the Mission bells calling the Indians to evening prayers. In a few minutes Josef sat before the fire, the good Padre himself smiling a greeting. No man was asked at the Mission who he was or why he had come, for each was welcome, in the name of God, to meals, a bed, and whatever he needed for his comfort.

Other travelers gathered around the blaze, but Josef sat apart, eating the beans and bread brought to him by a little Indian boy. All but he were cheerful and merry as they questioned the Padre about the Indians under his care and the fine gardens and fields of the Mission. At last Josef rose and silently tiptoed to the door of the church. There, before a picture of the Christ Child in his mother's arms, burned the four candles in their silver candlesticks.

Josef returned to the fire muttering, "I wish to sleep now." The Padre bowed his head, and answered, "May God bless thy slumbers. The boy will show thee thy room."

When the little Indian had lighted him to the tiny room and he was alone, he looked around carefully to discover whether it would be possible to escape quietly in the night with the candlestick. Nothing could be easier, for the room was without a door and opened out on the grass-plot behind the church. Within the room the only furniture was a bed and a small table. On the table stood a bowl of the rough kind of pottery made by the Indians.

As Josef set the candle down on the table the light gleamed on something bright. He looked closer and was amazed to find the bowl half filled with copper and silver coins. His first thought was that the last man who slept in the room had put this money on the table and then forgotten it. He started eagerly to pour the coins into his pocket, but they made such a jangling that he was frightened. He thought the Padre might hear, and of course would immediately take possession of all his wealth. As he handled the treasure very softly he noticed letters scratched in the sides of the bowl. Holding it close to the light, he read:

"Let him who stands in greatest need take from this bowl and go forth in peace."

Josef read these words over and over before he realized their meaning. The money was kept there so that any guest who was very poor might help himself. No one had counted it before he, Josef, had come, and no one would count it after he departed. He might take only one small copper—or none—or the entire bowlful, and still he was free to go away with the Padre's blessing, having received a night's lodging, good food and money—and himself given nothing.

For a long time Josef sat on the bed and thought about this. There was no reason why he should not put the money with the one peso already in his pocket—and perhaps take the candlestick besides. His need was certainly great. Had he not lost all his cattle, failed to find the gold, and stood now without a thing in the world except one coin and a few clothes? The Padre had meant it for such as he. As for the candlestick—well, he would leave the candlestick. It was wicked to steal from the church. He was young and strong and could find work easily. He would only take part of the money from the bowl. But first he would sleep.

Josef lay on his back, wide awake and quiet. Since he had decided not to steal the candlestick he felt as though a load had been lifted from his heart. He stroked the great muscles of his arms and thought, "How strong I am!" The words on the bowl, "Who stands in greatest need," kept running through his head. After all, with strength like his, why should he take the Padre's money? Others would need it more.

He turned over and closed his eyes, but the face of the good Padre came continually before him.

Suddenly Josef leaped from his bed. He searched hurriedly in his trousers pocket for the one silver peso and dropped it with a loud clink into the bowl. It would be for those whose need was greater than his. With a smile he lay down again and fell asleep.[5]

Poem:

> I would be true, for there are those who trust me;
> I would be pure, for there are those who care;
> I would be strong, for there is much to suffer;
> I would be brave, for there is much to dare.

I would be friend of all—the foe, the friendless;
I would be giving, and forget the gift;
I would be humble, for I know my weakness;
I would look up, and laugh, and love, and lift.

I would be learning, day by day, the lessons
My heavenly Father gives me in his Word;
I would be quick to hear his lightest whisper,
And prompt and glad to do the things I've heard.
—Howard Arnold Walter

PRAYER:
Our Father, as we wait in thy presence, speak to us. Free us from our narrow selves; take from our lives anything that keeps us from being vessels fit for thy use. Reveal our weaknesses and help us to overcome them. Give us a vision of the person we can become. Grant us courage to speak the truth, to be honest in everything we do, to keep our lives pure, always to do what is right. As our lives touch others, help us to relieve loneliness, to give encouragement and understanding. Forbid that we should be so wrapped up in ourselves that we fail to see the needs of others. Lead us every step of the way; guide our thoughts and actions. Through Christ we pray. AMEN.

HYMN: "O Son of Man, Thou Madest Known" or
"God, Who Touchest Earth with Beauty"

BENEDICTION:
May the peace of God that passeth all understanding keep your hearts and minds through Christ Jesus our Lord. AMEN.

AROUND THE YEAR
WITH GOD

SERVICE 20

OPENING CLOSED DOORS
(*Brotherhood Day*)

Christians believe that God created all men of one flesh and blood, and all are brothers regardless of race, nationality, religion, or social rank. Since God is the creator of all men and is a loving God, he values all men alike. Yet it is evident that some people are accepted and others are excluded. Americans have been criticized for believing in democracy but failing to practice it in their interracial dealings.

It is well for junior highs to face the problem of achieving friendly relations with people of all races. The following suggestions indicate obstacles that stand in the way of brotherhood:

Prejudice of people whose background is different

Ignorance of problems and needs of people of other races

Hate engendered by past injustices

Pride of race or nation

Suggested steps toward achieving brotherhood:

Invite exchange students from other countries to speak to group

Invite students from other countries into homes

Discover ways of helping Christian youth of other countries

Strive to live as brothers with people irrespective of race or status

PRELUDE: "Prelude in G Minor" by Bach

CALL TO WORSHIP:

Beloved, let us love one another:

For love is of God;

And every one that loveth is born of God, and knoweth God.[1]

123

HYMN: "Spirit of God, Descend upon My Heart" or
"Jesus, Thou Joy of Loving Hearts"

INVOCATION:

O Lord, reveal thyself to us; help us to know what is right; strengthen our wills that we may choose the good and refuse the evil. Deepen our love for thee; make us instruments in thy hands to serve where the need is greatest. In Jesus' name we pray. AMEN.

SCRIPTURE:

Ye are the salt of the earth: but if the salt have lost his savour, wherewith shall it be salted? It is thenceforth good for nothing, but to be cast out, and to be trodden under foot of men.

Ye are the light of the world. A city that is set on an hill cannot be hid.

Neither do men light a candle, and put it under a bushel, but on a candlestick; and it giveth light unto all that are in the house.

Let your light so shine before men, that they may see your good works, and glorify your Father which is in heaven.

Ye have heard that it hath been said, Thou shalt love thy neighbour, and hate thine enemy.

But I say unto you, Love your enemies, bless them that curse you, do good to them that hate you, and pray for them which despitefully use you, and persecute you.

Be ye therefore perfect, even as your Father which is in heaven is perfect.[2]

POEM:

> Gather us in, thou Love, that fillest all;
> Rend each man's temple veil, and bid it fall,
> Gather our rival faiths within thy fold;
> That we may know that thou hast been of old.
>
> Gather us in: we worship only thee;
> In diverse forms a common soul we see;
> In varied names we stretch a common hand;
> In many ships we seek one spirit-land.
>
> .   .   .   .
>
> Some seek a Father in the heavens above;
> Some crave a spirit vast as life and love;

OPENING CLOSED DOORS

Some ask a human image to adore;
Within thy mansions we have all and more.[3]
—Edward Dearle

LEADER:

We will hear the story of the "Little Professor of Piney Woods," who dedicated himself that the boys and girls of the Black Belt might have greater opportunities and a more abundant life.

STORY:

THE LITTLE PROFESSOR OF PINEY WOODS

Laurence Clifton Jones, the only Negro in his class at the University of Iowa, was a favorite of teachers and pupils alike. At graduation he turned down attractive offers in order to serve his race in a backward section of Mississippi. He selected the Piney Woods area in the Black Belt, twenty-two miles southeast of Jackson.

When he arrived there in 1909, most of the Negroes were sharecroppers working for a bare existence. He had grown up in St. Joseph, Missouri, where his father owned a hotel barbershop. This was a new experience to see people living in one-room shacks with no windows. But he was convinced that people could be taught to help themselves and eventually get rid of poverty and ignorance.

Jones met with indifference on every hand when he began talking about a school for Negroes. A white man to whom he appealed for help remarked, "There's no need trying to start a school for the colored; we have enough trouble trying to keep a white school going."

Undaunted, Jones called a meeting of the people of the community. He told of his plans: in addition to reading and writing the boys would be taught various trades; they would learn to farm, to raise stock, to conserve and market their produce. The girls would learn to cook, sew, teach, or do secretarial work. Religion would be taught, but no particular creed.

When Jones urged everyone present to support the school, the white men came forward with bills and the Negroes with quarters, dimes, and nickels. Others with no money pledged to give produce or labor. With this the school started, and three boys came on the first day. A Bible and a few farm journals were the textbooks.

Since there was not enough money to start a building, the classes were held in a field near a dilapidated cabin. Jones opened the school by singing and reading the Scriptures. Other pupils drifted in until there were fifty enrolled by the time winter began. They still met in the field, and the boys cut wood to keep a fire going.

Jones called on Edward Taylor, a former slave, the owner of the cabin in the field. He talked about the school and asked to use the cabin. Taylor inquired, "What are you teaching?" Jones replied, "At present I am teaching the boys to read and write, but I want to teach them to farm, raise stock, shoe horses, make brooms, and do other useful work. I want to train them to do skillful labor, take a pride in their work, build better homes, save a little, and get rid of ignorance and superstition."

The former slave became interested at once. He said, "I'll tell you what I will do. I will give you that old cabin and the forty acres around it and fifty dollars. By the looks of you, you could use it for food, if not for the school." Walking over to a drawer, he took out fifty one-dollar bills and gave them to the professor saying, "I'll fix you a deed for the forty acres."

Jones realized that a boarding school was necessary, for some pupils came from a distance. He called on John Webster, a sawmill owner, who gave ten thousand feet of lumber for a building. The pupils cleared the land, and the men of the community put up a two-story building that served as a dormitory and classrooms for the eighty-five pupils now enrolled.

The professor lectured in many places, telling of the school, and money began coming in. On one of these trips he met Gracie Allen, who was soliciting funds for a Kentucky college. Fortunately for him she was willing to marry him and share his task. She taught, carried on extension work with the women, and organized a chorus to further advertise the school.

Jones spent the summers in the North, speaking at civic clubs, churches, or wherever an opportunity was offered. As he told of the needs of the school, there was a ready response. His enthusiasm and determination won supporters and brought in enough money to keep the school going.

Less than 10 per cent of the pupils could pay any tuition, but no one was turned away for lack of funds. Those who could not pay brought a calf, a pig, chickens, or produce, and worked to pay the remainder. Each pupil was taught two trades, so if work was scarce in one, he could turn to the other. The school has never departed from its original purpose of opening doors of opportunity to the children of the poor.

Finally a great change came to the Piney Woods area. Today as one drives through this section, it is easy to pick out the farmers who have attended the Little Professor's school. Their homes are painted; crops are rotated; pure-bred cattle are grazing in the fields. Instead of a meager living, family life is enriched, boys and girls are educated, and poverty and ignorance will disappear from Piney Woods.

Commencement at this school is different from that of any other school. Instead of long speeches, a boy speaks a few minutes, takes off his cap and gown, and demonstrates the trade he has learned. A pig is brought in, and he vaccinates it for cholera. In like manner a girl talks a few minutes and makes a garment or cans tomatoes as the audience watches with interest. Each graduate displays an article that she has made from inexpensive material.

The school is quite different from its humble beginnings of forty-five years ago. There are now five hundred students and a $750,000 plant on a sixteen-acre campus. There are well-equipped workshops, a modern dairy, a farm, orchards, and a staff of forty well-trained and devoted teachers. An endowment has been set up that ensures the future of the school, but money will still need to be raised each year to pay current expenses. Jones still insists that each student be taught to work with his hands, so that he will always be able to earn a living.

Laurence Jones, now past seventy years of age, keeps going at a rate that would exhaust a younger man. When the whites and Negroes met recently to honor him as founder of the school, Governor Hugh White spoke of Jones as "one of the first citizens of Mississippi." When the superintendent of public instruction asked, "How did you keep going through the early years of struggle?" Jones replied, "I kept on praying as if everything depended on God, and kept on working as if everything depended on me. You can't get discouraged if you do that."

POEM:

> Dear Master, in whose life I see
> All that I long and fail to be;
> Let thy clear light for ever shine
> To shame and guide this life of mine.
>
> Though what I dream and what I do
> In my poor days are always two,
> Help me, oppressed by things undone,
> O Thou, whose dreams and deeds were one.
> —JOHN HUNTER

LEADER:

We appreciate men like Dr. Laurence Jones, who put selfish interests in the background and the needs of others first in his life. Through his effort and those who worked with him a new world of opportunity has been opened to the boys and girls of the Piney Woods area. He has given generously that these students may enter into an abundant life and be prepared for useful service. In our offering today we make it possible for others to have these privileges.

Let us remember the words of the apostle Paul as he said, "Every man according as he purposeth in his heart, so let him give; not grudgingly, or of necessity: for God loveth a cheerful giver.[4]

OFFERING[5]

RESPONSE:

> Grant us, Lord, the grace of giving
> With a spirit, large and free,
> That ourselves and all our living
> We may offer unto thee.

HYMN: "O Brother Man, Fold to Thy Heart Thy Brother" or "Where Cross the Crowded Ways of Life"

PRAYER:

Our Father, we thank thee for men like Dr. Laurence Jones who are laboring to wipe out ignorance and superstition among all races. Help us to see the needs and to be concerned about the problems of other races. May we share their burden, encourage and help them to make the most of their skill and ability, and remove obstacles from their way. If we have prejudice toward any people, help us to get rid of it. Forgive us for the times when we have failed to carry out good impulses. Help us to realize that Jesus was concerned about the poor and that all persons are important in thy sight. In Jesus' name we pray. AMEN.

BENEDICTION:

> The Lord bless thee and keep thee;
> The Lord make his face shine upon thee, and be gracious unto thee;
> The Lord lift up his countenance upon thee, and give thee peace.

SERVICE 21

AN URGENT REQUEST
(*Universal Bible Sunday*)

On the second Sunday in December we observe Universal Bible Sunday. The leader for this occasion should have the material ahead of time so as to make it his own. If worship is presented reverently and effectively, it will challenge the group to turn to their Bibles as a guide in daily living. It will mean much if they can be helped to form the habit of regular Bible reading.

There are many interests bidding for the time of junior highs, so unless parents and teachers help them to appreciate the Bible, they miss a part of their religious heritage. Since the best of English literature is saturated with references to the Bible, youth must have at least a partial knowledge of it in order to understand the literature.

Early in November order Bible-reading bookmarks with scripture selections for daily reading from Thanksgiving to Christmas. These may be secured from the American Bible Society, Department 5, 450 Park Avenue, New York 22, N.Y. There is no charge so order enough for everyone and share with other church groups.

The center of worship may be an open Bible with candles or with a bowl of flowers. If there is a religious bookstore near, it is well to check with it for suitable material for centers of worship.

PRELUDE: Hymn tune "Bread of Life"

CALL TO WORSHIP:
> O Word of God Incarnate,
> O Wisdom from on high,
> O Truth unchanged, unchanging,
> O Light of our dark sky:
> We praise thee for the radiance

129

That from the hallowed page,
A lantern to our footsteps,
Shines on from age to age.
—WILLIAM WALSHAM HOW

HYMN: "A Glory Gilds the Sacred Page" or
"Lamp of Our Feet"

PRAYER:
O Lord, open our lips that we may praise thee, inspire our hearts
that we may love thee, and direct our thoughts that we may worship
thee. We thank thee for the Bible, for it is a guide to us in daily
living. May we turn to it daily and find in its pages thy will for our
lives. AMEN.

SCRIPTURE:
Thy word have I hid in mine heart, that I might not sin against
thee. . . .
I will meditate in thy precepts, and have respect unto thy ways.
I will delight myself in thy statutes: I will not forget thy word. . . .
Teach me, O Lord, the way of thy statutes; and I shall keep it unto
the end.
Give me understanding, and I shall keep thy law; yea, I shall ob-
serve it with my whole heart. . . .
Thy word is a lamp unto my feet, and a light unto my path. . . .
Continue thou in the things which thou hast learned and hast
been assured of, knowing of whom thou hast learned them; and that
from a child thou hast known the holy scriptures, which are able
to make thee wise unto salvation through faith which is in Christ
Jesus. All scripture is given by inspiration of God, and is profitable
for doctrine, for reproof, for correction, for instruction in righteousness: that the man of God may be perfect, throughly furnished
unto all good works.[1]

LEADER:
During the early days in America when the missionaries were
sent out to carry the gospel to the American Indians, there were
many difficulties to overcome. Because of the treatment received
from the white man the Indians were hostile and refused to accept
the message of the missionaries. There was another obstacle to overcome: the language of the Indians had not been put into writing,

and it was many years before it was possible to translate the Bible into their language.

We will hear the story of the Nez Percés Indians' long trip to get a copy of the Bible in their own language.

STORY:

THE WHITE MAN'S BOOK OF HEAVEN

When the white explorers first came to the western slope of the Rocky Mountains, winter had already begun. They were received in a friendly manner by the Nez Percés Indians and remained with them until the snow melted and travel was again possible.

During these months of the white man's visit the Indians tried to figure out how he was able to do such wonderful things. They had many questions to ask about the guns and a book that he carried. The Indians decided that his gun was more powerful than their bows and arrows. Finally they came to the conclusion that the Book of Heaven, as they called the Bible, gave the white man his magic power. They were quite eager to find out how they could get this book.

Replying to their questions, the explorers explained as best they could about God and the Bible, but there were many English words that were not found at all in the Indian language. This made it difficult to convey a clear idea of the Great Spirit and the Book of Heaven. After the travelers departed, the Indians were still unsatisfied, and they sought a way to find out more about the white man's book.

In a council meeting in 1832 the tribe selected four Indian braves to go to St. Louis, Missouri, to get a copy of the wonderful book. This journey of more than two thousand miles over an unmarked trail through enemy country was a hazardous undertaking. After several months of travel, early one morning the Indian braves reached the frontier town of St. Louis. Without looking to the right or left they marched single file to the headquarters of General William Clark. It was evident that they had come a long distance, for their moccasins were thin and their blankets threadbare.

Several days passed before an Indian was located who could talk with the newcomers. Finally General Clark learned that they had come to get a copy of the Bible about which the white explorers had talked during their stay with the Indians in the Northwest. The General explained that the book had not been written in the Indian language. Still they waited, for they had been ordered to stay until they got the book. They tarried for another six months, asking questions daily about the Great Spirit and the Book of Heaven.

Finally two of the older braves, worn out from the long journey, became ill and died. At last the younger men made ready for the return trip over the long trail. On the evening before departure they sat down to a great feast prepared for them. General Clark explained that since their language had not been put into writing, it would take a long time to get the Bible printed for them to read. He promised to do all that was possible to get the book for them.

In reply one of the braves expressed their disappointment, saying, "I came to you over the long trail of many moons from the setting sun. I made my way with strong arms through enemies and strange lands that I might carry much back to my people. I go back to them with both arms broken and empty. My people sent me to get the white man's Book of Heaven. You took me to where you worship the Great Spirit with candles, and the book was not there. You showed me pictures of heaven and of the good land beyond, but the book was not among them. When I tell my people after one more snow in the big council that I did not bring the book, no word will be spoken by our old men or by our young warriors. One by one they will rise and go out in silence. My people will die in darkness and go a long path to their hunting grounds. No white man will go with them, and there will be no white man's book to make the way plain."

The story of the Indian's long journey for the Bible was told in several church papers. The result was that the various denominations set about to send missionaries to the Indians. Jason Lee and Marcus Whitman were sent to the Oregon Territory, and others followed.

The journey of the Indian braves over the long trail was not in vain. Finally the Nez Percés Indians not only had the Bible in their language, but also missionaries were sent to explain it to them and answer their questions about God.[2]

POEM:

> The heavens declare thy glory, Lord;
>   In every star thy wisdom shines;
> But when our eyes behold thy Word,
>   We read thy Name in fairer lines.

> The rolling sun, the changing light,
>   And nights and days, thy power confess;

AN URGENT REQUEST

But the blest Volume thou hast writ
 Reveals thy justice and thy grace.

Nor shall thy spreading gospel rest
 Till through the world thy truth has run;
Till Christ has all the nations blest
 That see the light, or feel the sun.

The noblest wonders here we view
 In souls renewed, and sins forgiven:
Lord, cleanse my sins, my soul renew,
 And make thy Word my guide to heaven.
 —Isaac Watts

LEADER:

The Bible was the first book ever printed and is still the most widely read book. Over fifty million copies of the Bible or portions of it are sold or given away each year by the various Bible societies or other firms in this and other countries. Through present-day translations nine tenths of the world's population may read the Bible or parts of it in their own language.

The early settlers of our country turned to the Bible as a guide for daily living. Our American way of life comes largely from the inspiration of this book. If we cherish our way of life and want to keep it, we should not only know the truths found in the Bible but live by them daily.

Let us repeat in unison the Beatitudes that Jesus gave in the Sermon on the Mount:

"Blessed are the poor in spirit: for theirs is the kingdom of heaven.

Blessed are they that mourn: for they shall be comforted.

Blessed are the meek: for they shall inherit the earth.

Blessed are they which do hunger and thirst after righteousness: for they shall be filled.

Blessed are the merciful: for they shall obtain mercy.

Blessed are the pure in heart: for they shall see God.

Blessed are the peacemakers: for they shall be called the children of God.

Blessed are they which are persecuted for righteousness' sake: for theirs is the kingdom of heaven.

Blessed are ye, when men shall revile you, and persecute you, and shall say all manner of evil against you falsely, for my sake.

Rejoice, and be exceeding glad: for great is your reward in heaven: for so persecuted they the prophets which were before you." [3]

PRAYER:

Our Father, we are grateful for the writers of the Bible, who lived close to thee and were inspired to write the various books of the Bible. We are thankful for the translators, who labored long hours and many were persecuted that we might have the Bible in our language. We are grateful that we live in a free country; help us to value the blessings that we enjoy. Help us to study the Bible, follow its teachings in our daily lives, and pass on its truths to those who come after us. Help us to share the scriptures with those who are not able to read. In Jesus' name we pray. AMEN.

OFFERING

LEADER:

The offering today will go to the American Bible Society to help make portions of the Scriptures available to others who do not have the Bible in their own language.[4]

HYMN: "Break Thou the Bread of Life" or
"A Charge to Keep I Have"

BENEDICTION:

The Lord bless us and keep us as thy own, and fill our hearts with thy love. AMEN.

SERVICE 22

SHARING THE GOOD NEWS
(*Missions Sunday*)

Every fourth Sunday is set aside as Missions Sunday in some denominations. The Joint Commission on Missionary Education representing the various denominations selects the home and foreign fields for study each year. It is inspiring to know that all age groups of the many Protestant churches are cooperating in study and worship and making plans to meet some of the needs of people in these areas. Joint textbooks are written that all groups may use.

Following the Resurrection the disciples had greater courage and spoke out boldly in their preaching. Christ had deeper meaning for them because his spirit ruled their lives. When Christ comes into our lives, it makes a difference. Not only are our lives changed, but we have a desire to tell others about the experience.

The command that Christ gave to go and make disciples of all nations was not limited to those who followed him during his ministry, but it comes to us today. If we take him seriously, accept the challenge of his life, we will want to win others to his cause. Not everyone can go as a missionary, but those who cannot go may help to send others. Helping to support workers with gifts and prayers is an effective way of obeying this command.

It would be appropriate to use a large globe of the world in a center of worship containing the picture "Jesus Calling the Fishermen" by Zimmermann or "Go Preach" by Burnand.

PRELUDE: Hymn tune "National Hymn"

CALL TO WORSHIP:
I have set thee to be a light of the Gentiles,
That thou shouldest be for salvation unto the ends of the earth. . . .

135

From the rising of the sun even unto the going down of the same my name shall be great among the Gentiles.[1]

HYMN: "We've a Story to Tell to the Nations" or
"Forward Through the Ages"

LEADER:
As we think of missions, what did Jesus say about the need for carrying the gospel to others?

FIRST BOY:
The harvest truly is plenteous, but the labourers are few. Pray ye therefore the Lord of the harvest, that he will send forth labourers into his harvest.

LEADER:
Did Jesus show concern for those who had not heard the gospel?

SECOND BOY:
Other sheep I have, which are not of this fold: them also I must bring, and they shall hear my voice; and there shall be one fold, and one shepherd.

LEADER:
What did Jesus say of the response of these people to the message?

FIRST GIRL:
They shall come from the east, and from the west, and from the north, and from the south, and shall sit down in the kingdom of God.

LEADER:
What promise did Jesus give to those who carried the gospel to others?

SECOND GIRL:
All power is given unto me in heaven and in earth. Go ye therefore, and teach all nations, baptizing them in the name of the Father, and of the Son, and of the Holy Ghost: teaching them to observe all things whatsoever I have commanded you: and, lo, I am with you alway even unto the end of the world.

SHARING THE GOOD NEWS

LEADER:

Did the early disciples preach to the Gentiles?

FIRST BOY:

Then Peter opened his mouth, and said, Of a truth I perceive that God is no respector of persons: but in every nation he that feareth him, and worketh righteousness, is accepted with him.[2]

LEADER:

The command comes to us today just as it did to the early Christians. Those of us who cannot go into other countries to carry the gospel can have a part by helping to send others. The offering today will go to missions. Our giving will be one way of helping to spread the gospel to many countries.

OFFERING

PRAYER:

We remember the words of Jesus when he said, It is more blessed to give than to receive. Accept the gifts we bring and also ourselves to be used in thy service. We pray for those in faraway places who have no one to teach them. Speak to us and open our hearts to the needs of people everywhere for a more abundant life. In Jesus' name. AMEN.

HYMN: "O Zion, Haste" or
"Christ for the World We Sing"

LEADER:

As we hear the story of William Carey, the father of modern missions, let us notice the many obstacles that he had to overcome in order to preach the gospel to the people in India.

STORY:

FROM COBBLER TO MISSIONARY

William Carey, the cobbler, propped his Bible in front of him and studied as he repaired shoes. One of his favorite passages was the command Jesus gave to his disciples, "Go ye into all the world, and preach the gospel." At that time there was little mission work done by the churches, but Carey believed that this command applied to all Christians everywhere. He felt the need so keenly that he talked with the people who came into his shop and spoke about it to groups wherever there was a chance.

Because of poverty in his home Carey's schooling ended when he was twelve years of age. But he taught himself Latin, Greek, and Hebrew so that he could read the Bible in these languages. At twenty-six years of age he was ordained a minister in the Baptist Church and kept on speaking on missions, his favorite theme. In May, 1792, at an annual meeting at Nottingham, England, he spoke of the need of sending the gospel to every creature. As a result the Baptist Missionary Society was formed, and money began coming in for missions.

At that time the idea of missions was unpopular, and many opposed Carey. On one occasion when he preached, a member in the group broke in saying, "Sit down, young man; when God gets ready to convert the heathen, he will do it without your help or mine!" Undaunted by this the young minister went on preaching and trying to interest others in missions.

When no one volunteered to go as a missionary, it was such a personal matter with Carey that he offered himself and enlisted a young doctor to go with him. Within a year he and his family, Dr. John Thomas and his wife, sailed for India. Their work began at Serampore, the only place in that country that was open to missionaries.

In spite of many problems Carey pushed ahead. During the first year when his wife was ill, their son had died, most of his money was gone, but he did not give up. The people also refused to listen to his preaching. The East India Company ordered him either to leave India or to make his stay legal by working for them. There was nothing for him to do but to go to work in the indigo factory, but at night he kept on with his work of translating the Bible into the language of the people.

The work in the factory proved to be a blessing in disguise, because it gave Carey a chance to learn the language and know the people better. The people were surprised to find him kind, considerate, and helpful. Never before had they known kindness from any Europeans. Although it took seven years to win his first convert to Christianity, he eventually became very effective as a teacher and translator of the Bible into the languages and dialects of the people.

Carey also taught in the government school. Other helpers were sent to assist him from England, among them an experienced printer.

Then the young missionary was able to set up his own printing shop and publish Bibles and other Christian literature in the language of the people.

On one occasion when Carey was away from home, a fire destroyed his printing plant and some of his translations. Instead of being discouraged he said, "We will improve the translations and build a better plant." Then he appealed to the British Bible Society for aid, and money was sent to rebuild and equip another plant. Eventually he brought out the Bible in thirty-two languages and dialects, thus making it known to the people in various sections of the country.

With the money coming from the sale of the Bibles, Carey opened up mission work in many centers and built schools, hospitals, and churches. This humble workman, a cobbler in England, was later known as the father of modern missions. His enthusiasm spread until other denominations began to feel a greater need for sharing the gospel with people of other countries. His motto, "Attempt great things for God; expect great things of God," carried him through many trying situations.

POEM:

> God of the nations, hear our call;
> Thou who art Father of us all,
> Show us our part in thy great plan
> For the vast brotherhood of man.
>
> Let us with earnestness of youth
> Care only for pursuit of truth.
> O may we feel thy guidance still
> And heed the impulse of thy will!
>
> Thus, as thy Kingdom cometh here,
> Shall it throughout the world draw near;
> And loyalty to country then
> Shall reach out to include all men.[3]
>
> —VERA CAMPBELL

PRAYER:

Our Father, we thank thee for the gift of thy son to the world. Help us better to understand his teachings and what thou dost expect of us. We are grateful for the privilege of sharing in the work of the missionaries. Give to them strength for their tasks, and may they have thy spirit guiding them when the demands are great and the results are meager. Be very near to all who teach and to those who listen. Hasten the day when all people shall bow before thee and worship thee in deed and in truth. May thy kingdom come in the hearts of people everywhere and nations learn to live peaceably; through Jesus our Master we pray. AMEN.

HYMN: "The Whole Wide World for Jesus" or
"The Morning Light Is Breaking" or
"Lead On, O King Eternal"

BENEDICTION:
May the peace of God that passeth all understanding guard your hearts and minds through Christ our Lord. AMEN.

SERVICE 23

ONE LIFE TO GIVE
(*Missions Sunday*)

PRELUDE: Hymn tune "Duke Street"

CALL TO WORSHIP:
  One is your Father, which is in heaven. . . .
  And all ye are brethren.
  [God] hath made of one blood all nations of men for to dwell
    on all the face of the earth, . . .
  Therefore all things whatsoever ye would that men should do to
    you, do ye even so to them: . . .
  O come, let us worship and bow down: let us kneel before the
    Lord our maker.[1]

HYMN: "The Kingdom Come, O Lord" or
        "Jesus Shall Reign Where'er the Sun"

POEM:
  Hold high the torch!
  You did not light its glow—
  'Twas given you by other hands, you know.
  'Tis yours to keep it burning bright,
  Yours to pass on when you no more need light;
  For there are other feet that we must guide,

  . . . .
  Hold high the torch!

141

You did not light its glow—
'Twas given you by other hands, you know.
I think it started down its pathway bright,
The day the Maker said: "Let there be light."
And he once said, who hung on Calvary's tree—
"Ye are the light of the world." . . . Go! . . . Shine—for me.

—AUTHOR UNKNOWN

SCRIPTURE:

The Spirit of the Lord God is upon me; because the Lord hath anointed me to preach good tidings unto the meek; he hath sent me to bind up the brokenhearted, to proclaim liberty to the captives, and the opening of the prison to them that are bound; to proclaim the acceptable year of the Lord, . . . to comfort all that mourn; . . . to give unto them beauty for ashes, the oil of joy for mourning, the garment of praise for the spirit of heaviness; . . . that he might be glorified.

As Moses lifted up the serpent in the wilderness, even so must the Son of man be lifted up: that whosoever believeth in him should not perish, but have eternal life.

For God so loved the world, that he gave his only begotten Son, that whosoever believeth in him should not perish, but have everlasting life.[2]

PRAYER:

O God, who hast revealed thyself through thy Son, through thy Word, and through followers of thine, help us to have a clear vision of thy purpose for us. We are thankful for every influence that has led us to desire the Christian way of life. Show us what we can do to share the gospel with those who have not heard the good news. Accept our gifts and lead us into paths of service that will help to bring thy kingdom nearer; through Jesus Christ our Lord. AMEN.

The offering today will go to the support of missionaries. (Mention the field.)

OFFERING:

Toyohiko Kagawa was converted to Christianity through the effort of Dr. Myers, a Presbyterian missionary to Japan. You will hear the story of this great leader who has lived by the spirit of Christ since his conversion.

STORY:

TOYOHIKO KAGAWA—ENCHANTED BY LOVE

Toyohiko Kagawa's father was a wealthy man with great influence. When the boy was four years old, both parents died, and he was sent to live with his grandmother. Two of her sons had disappointed her, so she disliked the idea of having another boy put in her care. The lad felt that he was not wanted, and his childhood was filled with fear and abuse.

Toyohiko went to live with a wealthy uncle in Tokushima where he entered the Boys' Middle School, which would be grades seven to ten in the United States. Here he met a Christian teacher and two missionary families who were friendly to him. In order to improve his English, he joined the class in English of Dr. Meyers, a missionary.

The lad often visited the home of Dr. Meyers and through conversation discovered what it meant to have a Father in heaven. After memorizing the Sermon on the Mount, the boy was better able to understand what it meant to follow Christ. When the missionary encouraged Toyohiko to be a Christian, he accepted Christ and his way of life and from that time was confident of the loving care of a heavenly Father.

In spite of the uncle's opposition the boy felt that he must serve the poor. Hearing that unfortunate families in the slums lived in houses six feet square, he felt that he could no longer enjoy the luxury of his uncle's home. While he had a great desire for books and learning, he was eager to practice his beliefs. He was convinced that there should not be a gulf between what he believed and what he did.

He decided to study for the ministry at the Presbyterian College in Tokyo, rather than go to the Imperial University and prepare for a diplomatic career as his uncle desired. His refusal to accept his uncle's plan for his life brought about a complete break between them. This choice changed his future from that of being a member of the richest family in the province to that of being a penniless student.

Upset by the boy's decision, the uncle demanded, "If you do not leave the seminary at once, you need expect no more help from me." Teachers at the seminary came to his aid by securing a part-time job for him and donating money for food and clothing.

Kagawa had sympathy for the poor and lonely, even for deserted animals. One day he rescued a bedraggled pup from a gutter and brought it to his room. The other students protested, but he insisted that while anyone would give a home to a healthy, good-looking dog, no one would take care of a deserted animal unless he would do it. He not only brought a beggar to his room, but he gave away the money that was allowed him by the school, and he would give away his clothes whenever he found a beggar who needed them more than himself.

Whenever there was an unpopular cause, Toyohiko sponsored it. He became an ardent believer in the law of love, which, as he saw it, meant refusing to fight to gain one's end. He would not support the war in which his country was engaged. This brought down upon him the wrath of the entire student body and also many others.

Kagawa had never been strong, and his health was the constant concern of his friends. In the second year of his college career he became a victim of tuberculosis. He was sent to an isolated village on the seashore to try to recover his health. Before he was well, he insisted upon returning to school.

The strenuous life that he undertook afterward would have been difficult for one with perfect health. He spent the mornings at his studies, and every afternoon and evening he preached and carried on social work in the slums. Later in order to help those who had become Christians, he moved to the slums and lived with drunks, murderers, and castoffs.

He soon realized that preaching was not enough, that he would have to take action to help people caught in poverty, disease, and distress. He opened a free clinic, for disease was everywhere. He organized classes both morning and evening, and two hours of every day were reserved for street preaching. He continued to serve in the slums for four years and then came a chance to study at Princeton University and observe methods of carrying on social service in the United States.

Immediately upon his return to Japan he went back to the slums to live. The stories of his encounters with desperate and brutal people of the slums would fill volumes with exciting narrative. But Kagawa found that it was not well to spend all his time helping people, that he must make it possible for them to help themselves.

When Kagawa realized that new laws would have to be passed and conditions changed, he organized unions for laborers and farmers and started a movement to give the vote to all who could qualify. He started Bible classes in factories, and today thousands are studying because he encouraged them to discover value in Bible study. His goal is to lead the masses to accept Christ, make education available for the poor, and extend a chance for development for everyone.

After the war Kagawa helped to bring about the appointment of Christians as cabinet members and even helped to have a Christian appointed as prime minister to Japan. He always refused any positions of honor that were offered him; instead he urged that other Christians fill the offices, and to them he gave full support.

Kagawa believes that love is the greatest force in the world. He says, "Only before love do I bow in reverence." Whatever may be said in the future of him and his work, one thing is sure: it will have to be with one word—"love." [3]

POEM:

> I sought my soul,
>> But my soul I could not see.
> I sought my God,
>> But my God eluded me.
> I sought my brother,
>> And I found all three.
>> —AUTHOR UNKNOWN

PRAYER:

Dear Father of all mankind, help us to realize that people of all races are our brothers. Guide us as we try to know the problems of people in various countries and may we relate our message to their needs. Help us to train local leaders to carry on the work we are now doing so that Christian teaching ceases to be foreign to the people we serve. Give us a better understanding of what it means to follow Christ in daily living. Grant us strength to meet opposition with love, anger with patience, and selfishness with a concern for others, in the name of the Master of us all we pray. AMEN.

HYMN: "A Charge to Keep I Have" or
"At Length There Dawns the Glorious Day"

BENEDICTION:

O Lord, hasten the day when righteousness shall cover the earth as the waters cover the sea, and all people shall hear and heed thy message of love. AMEN.

SERVICE 24

A GIFT FROM MOTHERS
(Mother's Day)

As Mother's Day draws near, it would be advisable to lead junior highs to discover various ways of honoring their mothers. In addition to giving gifts and wearing a flower on the day set apart to honor mothers the group might discuss what could be done throughout the year to express love and appreciation, such as:

Learning to co-operate in family projects

Living according to standards set by the family

Striving to achieve one's best development

Since every person is affected by the religious tone of his family, fortunate are young people who can learn from examples in the home what it means to be a Christian. Junior highs may examine themselves by facing frankly the following questions:

Do we appreciate the values we receive from our families?

Have we made our adjustment to each member of the family?

Have we done our part in contributing to happy family living?

Have we assumed our share of responsibility?

What else might we do to show appreciation?

Are we giving our best to our families?

As a center of worship use a picture of a mother or of a family—for example, Whistler's "Arrangement in Gray and Black," or von Uhde's "Christ the Welcome Guest," or Lhermitte's "Among the Lowly."

PRELUDE: "Ave Maria" by Bach-Gounod

CALL TO WORSHIP:

Who can find a virtuous woman?
for her price is far above rubies.
The heart of her husband doth safely trust in her, . . .
She openeth her mouth with wisdom;

146

and in her tongue is the law of kindness.
She looketh well to the ways of her household,
    and eateth not the bread of idleness.
Her children arise up, and call her blessed.[1]

HYMN: "O Perfect Love" or
    "O Love Divine and Golden."

PRAYER:

O God, thou whose gracious presence blessed the home of Mary
and Martha, help us to make our hearts ready for thee. Enter into
our lives and abide with us. Bless our homes and help us to make of
them the kind of place where everything is filled with love and kindness. We thank thee for the love and care that our mothers gave to
us. Help us to remember the training which they gave and to live by
it. In Jesus' name. AMEN.

SCRIPTURE:

Beloved, let us love one another: for love is of God. . . .
Beloved, if God so loved us, we ought also to love one another. . . .
Honour thy father and thy mother: that thy days may be long upon
the land which the Lord thy God giveth thee. . . .
Children, obey your parents in all things: for this is well pleasing
unto the Lord.[2]

OFFERING

RESPONSE:

Bless thou the gifts our hands have brought;
    Bless thou the work our hearts have planned;
Ours is the faith, the will, the thought;
    The rest, O God, is in thy hand.
                                —SAMUEL LONGFELLOW

LEADER:

Miss Anna Jarvis of Philadelphia is credited with being the origi-
nator of Mother's Day. She selected a day in early May on which she
wore a white flower as a token of her love and devotion to her mother.
Her friends liked the idea so well that they urged her to plan a service
for the entire community. This was in 1908.

The idea spread and in 1914 Miss Jarvis called on a Representative
asking him to introduce a bill providing for a national observance of
Mother's Day. The resolution in part stated: "The service rendered in
the United States by the American mother is the greatest source of
the country's strength and inspiration; we honor ourselves and the

mothers of America when we do anything to give emphasis to the home as the fountainhead of the State."

The bill was passed, and the second Sunday in May has been observed as a national day of remembrance of mothers since that time.

In the story we shall hear of what Laurence Jones learned from his mother.

STORY:

THE BEST ADVICE I EVER HAD

I must have been quite young when I first heard it, for the quaint, old-fashioned phrase runs through all my childhood memories with the persistence of a familiar tune: "Willful waste makes woeful want, and you may live to see the day when you will say, 'Oh, how I wish I had the bread that once I threw away.'"

I hear the words spoken in my mother's soft voice as she worked in her quick, industrious fashion around the neat little house in St. Joseph, Missouri, where my sisters and I were born. Far from being the practical realist that those words suggest, my fragile, poetry-loving mother was a dreamer. But she knew that within that phrase lay the chance for her dreams, and mine, to come true.

At first the words meant literally the piece of bread and jam in my hand which I might have tossed aside uneaten. Later they meant money, for from the age of six I always had a job of some sort, and learned to save the pennies, dimes and quarters toward the dream of a college education.

At the University of Iowa, where I tended furnace and waited table to pay my way, waste came to mean time. Since I had only a few hours each day for study, I had to make up in extra concentration what I lacked in time. Consequently my lessons burned into my memory, and they did much to shape the course of my life.

When I finished college, waste suddenly took on a new important meaning: the possible waste of opportunity.

In 1907, the year of my graduation, comparatively few Negroes had a similar chance of formal education. Although I had tempting job offers which ranged from the insurance business to a subsidized career in musical comedy, it seemed to me that if I used my education for selfish profit, that too would be a form of "willful waste."

I decided to share my advantages with the neediest people of my race in the Black Belt of Mississippi. There was the most shocking waste of all: the waste of the human mind and soul. Men, women and children exhausted their bodies in the fields, making their living as farmers but having no knowledge of farming beyond the drudgery of chopping and picking cotton. Unable to read, write or figure, they had no way of knowing if what they were charged at the store was correct, or if their wages were paid in full. Winter diets were corn meal and dried peas, because the women had never learned how to can or preserve the summer yield from their gardens or the wild berries that grew at their doors.

My mother's phrase came sharply to mind. My job would be to begin at the bottom and teach them, first of all, how to save what pitiful little they had. I set up a school of practical education, to teach good work habits, sanitation, diversified farming, how to cook, can and sew. The dream that lay ahead of this practical saving was better living conditions, adequate schools and churches, and ultimately instruction in trades and professions.

Then, after almost 20 years of work, as Piney Woods began to take shape as a real school, with the beginnings of an adequate plant, a steady enrollment and nearly enough teachers, my wife died, leaving a void not only in my life but in the operation of the school in which she had played a vital role. The temptation to give way to personal grief was strong. But once again my mother's words echoed in my ears. Grief, too, was a luxury, a "willful waste," when 500 children were depending on me for their education, their chance to become useful citizens.

What is education, or civilization itself for that matter, but a form of saving? We harvest and keep the best of the world's ideas and inventions so that we may pass them along to the generations that follow.

My job in life has been to try to save human beings from the willful waste of ignorance and despair, and to help them take their places as competent citizens in tomorrow's world. It is a task that I would choose again, if I were young. It was motivated by these words which I share with you. I can vouch for the rewards they will bring.[3]

POEM:

> She loved her work and home and friends,
>   And treasured beauty in her heart,
> Rejoiced to share life's dividends
>   And freely do a woman's part.

Her God was on the path she trod,
Her heaven here on earth began;
Awhile she lived with man and God,
And now she lives with God and man.[4]
—CHAUNCEY R. PIETY

SPECIAL MUSIC: (sung as a solo to the tune "Somewhere A Voice Is Calling")

Mother, our hearts are singing
Love that is true;
Mother, the world is bringing
Tribute to you;
Mother, now young and tender,
Or grey and old,
God give you joys and gladness,
All you can hold.

Mother, the queen of childhood,
and stay of youth;
Mother, faithful and loyal,
Tested by truth;
Mother, we are confessing
Debts none can pay;
Mother, we pray God's blessing
On you alway.[5]
—CHAUNCEY R. PIETY

PRAYER:

Our Father, we thank thee for our homes, our mothers, for their love and care expressed in many ways, for their faith in us and their encouragement, and for their dreams and ideals for us. May their love for us lead us to strive to make the most of our opportunities. Help us to demand the best of ourselves in order to make their dreams come true. Give us strength as we try to learn self-control and make us patient as we discipline ourselves. Grant that we may live in such manner as to honor our mothers. In Jesus' name we pray. AMEN.

HYMN: "Happy the Home When God Is There" or
"I Would Be True."

BENEDICTION:

May the grace of our Lord Jesus Christ and the love of God and the fellowship of the Holy Spirit be with us evermore. AMEN.

SERVICE 25

SELF IN TRAINING
(*Race Relations Sunday*)

On the Sunday nearest February 12, the day set apart as Race Relations Sunday, we have the privilege of learning about Negro schools of our denomination. The counselor has the opportunity to help junior highs search their own minds to determine whether they are prejudiced against persons of any race. They may also realize that if they accept the fatherhood of God, the brotherhood of man follows.

It is advisable to present stories in worship services of distinguished members of the Negro race who have attained fame, such as Marian Anderson, the musical artist; Laurence Jones, the educator; Jackie Robinson, the athlete; George Washington Carver, the scientist; James Weldon Johnson, the writer; and others.

However, most teen-agers do not know personally such outstanding leaders. How do they feel toward the Negroes they do know? Do they think of them as neighbors? Do they appreciate their contribution as individual members of our society? Do they have a friendly attitude? Do teen-agers make an effort to get along with those of a different race?

Jesus stressed the value of human personality and the sacredness of each individual in the sight of God. Can the members of the group be led to think of all people as neighbors and show a Christian concern for all regardless of the color of skin?

Prelude: Hymn tune "Finlandia" by Jean Sibelius

Call to Worship:
> It is a good thing to give thanks unto the Lord,
>   and to sing praises unto thy name, O most High:

151

To shew forth thy lovingkindness in the morning,
and thy faithfulness every night. . . .
For thou, Lord, hast made me glad through thy work:
I will triumph in the works of thy hands.
O Lord, how great are thy works! and thy thoughts
are very deep.[1]

HYMN: "God of the Strong, God of the Weak" or
"Awake, Awake to Love and Work"

RESPONSIVE READING:
Leader: God is no respector of persons: but in every nation he that
feareth him, and worketh righteousness, is accepted with him.
Group: We bear the strain of earthly care,
But bear it not alone;
Beside us walks our Brother Christ
And makes our task his own.
Leader: But as touching brotherly love ye need not that I write unto
you: for ye yourselves are taught of God to love one another.
. . . For ye are all the children of God by faith in Christ
Jesus.
Group: The common hopes that make us men
Were his in Galilee;
The tasks he gives are those he gave
Beside the restless sea.
Leader: God is love; and he that dwelleth in love dwelleth in God,
and God in him. . . . We love him, because he first loved
us. . . . And this commandment we have from him, That he
who loveth God love his brother also.[2]
Group: Our brotherhood still rests in him,
The Brother of us all,
And o'er the centuries still we hear
The Master's winsome call.
—OZORA S. DAVIS

PRAYER:
Our Father, make us more sensitive to the needs of others and
may we show brotherly love to everyone. Grant that we may use our
talents to lead others to a more abundant life. May we be not only
listeners but doers of thy Word. Grant that we may become more
worthy of fellowship with thee. Strengthen us as we strive to serve
thee. In Jesus' name we pray. AMEN.

SELF IN TRAINING

LEADER:

We will hear the story of the first Negro who became a major league ball player.

STORY:

TROUBLE AHEAD NEEDN'T BOTHER YOU
Jackie Robinson

I'll never forget the day Branch Rickey, former President of the Brooklyn Dodgers, asked me to join his baseball organization. I would be the first Negro to play in organized baseball—that is, if I were good enough to make the grade.

Mr. Rickey's office was large and simply furnished. There were four framed pictures on the wall [among them one of Abraham Lincoln, who had pleaded for malice toward none]. . . . From behind his desk the big, powerful, bushy-browed Branch Rickey . . . mapped out to me his daring strategy to break the color line in major league baseball.

I was excited at the opportunity. It was a tremendous challenge. But was I good enough?

"Mr. Rickey," I said, "it sounds like a dream come true—not only for me but for my race. For seventy years there has been racial exclusion in big league baseball. There will be trouble ahead—for you, for me, for my people, and for baseball."

"Trouble ahead," Rickey rolled the phrase over his lips as though he liked the sound. "You know, Jackie, I was a small boy when I took my first train ride. On the same train was an old couple, also riding for the first time. We were going through the Rocky Mountains. The old man sitting by the window looked forward and said to his wife, 'Trouble ahead, Ma! We're high up over a precipice and we're gonna run right off.'

"To my boyish ears the noise of the wheels repeated 'Trouble-ahead-trouble-ahead. . . .' I never hear train wheels to this day but what I think of this. But our train course bent into a tunnel right after the old man spoke, and we came out on the other side of the mountain. That's the way it is with most trouble ahead in this world. Jackie—if we use the common sense and courage God gave us. But you've got to study the hazards and build wisely."

I've never forgotten that little story. It helped me through many of the rough moments I was to face in the future. I signed my con-

153

tract that day with a humble feeling of great responsibility. I prayed that I would be equal to the test.

"God is with us in this, Jackie," Mr. Rickey said quietly. "You know your Bible. It's good, simple Christianity for us to face realities and to recognize what we're up against. We can't go out and preach and crusade and bust our heads against a wall. We've got to fight out our problems together with tact and common sense."

To give me experience and seasoning, Mr. Rickey sent me the first year to play with the Montreal Royals, a farm club for the Brooklyn organization. I was the cause of trouble from the start—but we expected it. Pre-season exhibition games were canceled because of "mixed athletes," although the official reason was always different.

Some of my teammates may have resented me. If so, I didn't blame them. They had problems enough playing ball without being a part of a racial issue. I tried hard not to develop rabbit ears, a malady picked up by all athletes who are sensitive to abuse and criticism shouted from the fans.

One of my top thrills was my opening game for Montreal at Jersey City. The pressure was on and I was very nervous. But during that contest I slapped out four hits, including a home run. I couldn't have dreamed up a better start.

But as the season began to unroll game after game, my playing grew erratic. I was trying too hard. I knew I had to keep my temper bridled at every turn. Guarding so carefully against outbursts can put a damper on one's competitive spirit.

Every athlete at some time or other likes "to blow his top." It seldom does any harm and acts like a safety valve. A hitter in a slump may drive the ball deep to the infield, then leg it to first, sure that he has beaten the throw. The umpire calls him out. With this the frustrated athlete jerks off his cap, slams it on the ground and thunders all his pent-up irritations at the umpire. The crowd roars its approval or dislike depending on whether the player is on the home or visiting team. The umpire merely turns his back, and the ball player, after giving vent to his unhappiness, trots back to the bench feeling much better. It's all a part of the game.

But I didn't dare let loose this way. Many would have dubbed me a "hothead" and point to my outburst as a reason why Negroes should not play in organized baseball. This was one of the hardest problems I had to face.

As the season rolled along, however, the players became accustomed to me. My playing improved. When the season ended,

Montreal had won the Junior World Series. I admit proudly to winning the batting championship of the league with an average of .349.

On April 10, 1947, Branch Rickey made the announcement that gave me my greatest thrill. I was to join the Brooklyn Dodgers and become the first Negro to compete in the major leagues.

It was Montreal all over again, but this time the pressure was much greater, the competition keener, and the stakes tremendous. It wasn't a question so much of a Negro athlete making good as a big leaguer, but whether the whole racial question would be advanced or retarded.

Again I faced the same problems. An opposing player drove a hard grounder to the infield. When he crossed first base his spikes bit painfully into my foot. Accident or deliberate? Who can tell? But the first reaction of a competitive ball player is to double up fists and lash out. I saw a blinding red. It took every bit of my discipline to bridle my temper. But when my teammates rushed to my support in white hot anger, it gave me the warmest feeling I've ever felt. At that moment I belonged.

That year the Dodgers won the pennant. I was thrilled to know that my efforts were considered an important factor in winning. But I also cherished another triumph. Baseball as a whole had come to accept the Negro. Since then a number of Negroes . . . have developed into Major League stars. To make the grade they simply had to have the ability. As Mr. Rickey says, a champion is a champion in America, black or white.[3]

Never excuse yourself. Never pity yourself. Be a hard master to yourself—and be lenient to everybody else.—HENRY WARD BEECHER.

SCRIPTURE:

If any man among you seem to be religious, and bridleth not his tongue, but deceiveth his own heart, this man's religion is vain. Pure religion and undefiled before God and the Father is this, . . . to keep himself unspotted from the world.[4]

LEADER:

On Race Relations Sunday we can show that we believe all men are brothers. One way we can do this is by our attitude toward people of other races. Are we friendly, indifferent, or hostile to them? Do we treat everyone like we would like to be treated? In our offering today we have the privilege of giving to a Negro school of our denomination. This offering will help to provide better training for boys and girls in this school. (Name the school or college.)

OFFERING

POEM:

> Come forth, O Christian youth,
> A task before us lies;
> The world awaits the strength and zeal
> Which youthful heart supplies.
> We seek to win mankind
> To choose Christ's nobler way,
> And usher in true brotherhood
> For every man today.
>
> Stand firm, O Christian youth,
> With trust in God alone,
> That we may live our Christian faith
> And make Christ truly known.
> Be ours to show all men
> The path his feet have trod,
> To make all life a sacrament
> And holy unto God.
>
> Grow strong, O Christian youth,
> Be loyal, brave, and true,
> And strive with courage for the right
> In what we say and do.
> Thus may our words and deed
> Be worthy in God's sight,
> And manifest to all mankind
> His way of truth and light.
>
> Give all, O Christian youth,
> And naught from Christ withhold;
> His kingdom claims us for its own;
> His spirit keeps us bold!
> As pilgrims in the world
> Yet followers of the Way,
> God make us faithful citizens
> Till his eternal day.[5]

—MARY ELLEN JACKSON

PRAYER:

Our Father, help us to understand more fully the meaning of brotherhood. We are grateful for the example of those who have pioneered in friendly ways of living with other races. Help us to be willing to put the needs of others above our own. May we sympathize with the weak, the oppressed, and the handicapped. May we be willing to share with members of other races the same opportunity for an education. Help us to get rid of any hatred or prejudice that we might have toward anyone and learn how to be friendly and live as brothers with all races. Draw us closer to thee in bonds of love. In Jesus' name we pray. AMEN.

HYMN: "We Thank Thee, Lord, Thy Paths of Service Lead" or "Teach Us, O Lord, True Brotherhood"

BENEDICTION:

O Lord, dismiss us with thy blessing; watch over us while we are absent one from the other. AMEN.

SERVICE 26

THANKS BE TO GOD
(*Thanksgiving*)

Gratitude is one of the finest expressions of which a person is capable. Giving thanks regularly should be a definite part of Christian experience. The following questions may be a yardstick by which we check on the gratitude we feel for blessings we enjoy:

Are we grateful for all good things that come to us, or do we accept blessings as a matter of fact?

Are we shallow or insincere in our thanksgiving?

Do we express thanks to God as readily as we make requests?

Can we rejoice with a friend who receives a gift or has been honored, or does envy or jealousy creep in at such times?

If disappointed do we ask God to show us how to realize good from the experience?

When frustration comes, do we ask God to increase our faith that things will work out right, or do we complain and make others unhappy?

A worship center may be a cornucopia filled with fruit or other produce from the land. Arrange it on a table placed in the center front of the room. A small committee may be asked to write a litany of thanks for the occasion.

PRELUDE: Hymn tune "Hymn to Joy" Beethoven

CALL TO WORSHIP:
> O give thanks to the Lord, call on his name,
>   make known his deeds among the peoples!
> Sing to him, sing praises to him,
>   tell of all his wonderful works! [1]

HYMN: "Come, Ye Thankful People, Come" or
"We Plow the Fields and Scatter"

THANKS BE TO GOD

Our Father, we thank thee for the beauty which thou hast created; for food which strengthens our bodies and gives us energy to work and play; for our parents, brothers, and sisters; for our homes and all the comforts that we enjoy; for our country with all the privileges coming to us; for freedom, peace, and all the good things coming from thee. Grant that in this land of opportunity good will and brotherhood may abide in the hearts of all. In Jesus' name we pray. AMEN.

SCRIPTURE:

Make a joyful noise unto the Lord, all ye lands.

Serve the Lord with gladness: come before his presence with singing.

Know ye that the Lord he is God: it is he that hath made us, and not we ourselves; we are his people, and the sheep of his pasture.

Enter into his gates with thanksgiving, and into his courts with praise: be thankful unto him, and bless his name.

For the Lord is good; his mercy is everlasting; and his truth endureth to all generations. . . .

O give thanks unto the Lord; call upon his name: make known his deeds among the people.

Sing unto him, sing psalms unto him: talk ye of all his wondrous works.

Glory ye in his holy name: let the heart of them rejoice that seek the Lord.

Seek the Lord, and his strength: seek his face evermore.[2]

POEM:

> Our God, we thank thee for the world
> So wonderful and fair;
> And for the orchards, gardens, fields,
> And good things everywhere;
> And thanks for lakes and rivers,
> And mountains steep and high,
> And for the sun and moon so bright,
> And stars that fill the sky.
>
> We thank thee, God, for cities, towns,
> And plains and prairies too
> And thanks for farms and shops and mines,
> And flag, Red, White and Blue;
> Thanks, God, for homes, schools, churches,

And all kind folk that be,
And thanks for hope that we may live
Eternally with thee.[3]

—CHAUNCEY R. PIETY

LEADER:

We will hear the story of the first Thanksgiving.

STORY:

THE FIRST THANKSGIVING

More than 330 years ago a little ship sailed from a port in South England. That frail ship, ninety feet long and twenty feet wide, carried 120 passengers. Fighting its way for thirteen weeks through a rough sea, it was driven from its course by severe storms. At last, with its hull waterlogged and with food almost gone, it landed in a harbor in a strange, new world. From that ship, the Mayflower, landing at Plymouth, with a small group of Pilgrims, has come the ideals on which our nation was founded.

The Pilgrims were so poor that they had only one tenth of the money necessary for the trip across the Atlantic. It took twenty-three years to pay the rest, which they had borrowed from London bankers. They learned to live on food that was different—fish, wild game, nuts, or whatever they could get. They missed the comforts and security that they had left behind, but were willing to take the risks and face the dangers ahead.

Immediately this group of brave young men set out to build homes in the wilderness. They cleared the land, erected log cabins, and planted crops of grain before the winter began. They were probably afraid as they looked at the wilderness on three sides of them into which no white man had ever penetrated. They dreaded the winter, for which they were not prepared, but they had faith in God and courage to face the odds against them.

These early settlers had no material comforts and were hungry and cold most of the time. They did not blame anyone for no promises about the future had been made to them. They made their own decision to face hardships and dangers in order to worship God according to their own ideas. They did not want to be tools in the hands of rulers with no freedom of choice on their part.

At last their meager crops were gathered, and with plenty of wild game new hope and faith came to them. The courage which had enabled them to leave their homes now helped them to face the future unafraid. Their first thought was to express thanks to God for the blessings that had already come to them. So their governor set aside a special day when they would come together for fellowship and thanksgiving.

December 13, 1621, was the day selected by Governor Bradford. Four of the best riflemen were sent out to bring in the game for the meal. They returned with many turkeys and other wild game. Up to this time the women had had little chance to show their skill as cooks. Now there was plenty of food, and they enjoyed preparing the feast for the occasion.

The governor invited King Massasoit and ninety of his Indian braves to join them in the feast. They came all decked out in paint and feathers, bringing five deer to add to the banquet. As they sat down to the feast, which lasted three days, the Indians outnumbered the whites two to one. But the settlers were no longer afraid of them. The fear of hunger was also gone, and the future looked brighter, as they gave thanks to God for blessings showered upon them.

The first public building that the settlers erected was a church. They did not intend to forget God, from whom their help had come. They had a firm belief that God had no favorites, but that all people were his children. This idea was the driving force behind their struggle for freedom.

At this first Thanksgiving feast there were fifty-five men and women who offered up thanks to God. Forty-six of their number lay buried on the bluff overlooking the place where they landed. The survivors still faced hardships of another winter, possible sickness, and other dangers, but they were thankful to be free to think for themselves and to worship God as they pleased.

These settlers and others who followed them cleared forests, built highways, schools and churches, and founded our civilization. We are indebted to them for a rich heritage of freedom. We are enjoying the fruits of their labors, reaping where we have not sown.

LEADER:

The situation today is quite different from that of the early Pilgrims. Very few of us plant crops, tend the fields, and cultivate the grain. But let each of us in our own way thank God for our food that comes from many countries. Let us also thank him for those who labor day after day to produce this food. As we sit down to our Thanksgiving dinner, let us think of all the people in many countries

who worked that we might enjoy this meal, and let us ask God to
bless them.

POEM:

> Great God of nations, now to thee
>   Our hymn of gratitude we raise;
> With humble heart and bending knee
>   We offer thee our song of praise.
>
> Thy Name we bless, almighty God,
>   For all the kindness thou hast shown
> To this fair land the Pilgrims trod,
>   This land we fondly call our own.
>
> Here freedom spreads her banner wide
>   And casts her soft and hallowed ray;
> Here thou our fathers' steps didst guide
>   In safety thro' their dangerous way.
>
> Great God, preserve us in thy fear;
>   In danger still our guardian be;
> O spread thy truth's bright precepts here;
>   Let all the people worship thee.
>   —ALFRED A. WOODHULL

PRAYER:

Our Father, we thank thee for our forefathers who brought to this
country the ideals on which our nation was founded. We thank thee
that we are free to think for ourselves, to make our own decisions, and
to worship as we please. We pray for those who rule over us and
guide our nation. We thank thee for the faith of our forefathers. Help
us to feel that we must look to thee for help and for guidance. Give us
courage to face dangers today as fearlessly as did our ancestors. Lead
us in paths of peace, justice, and brotherhood. In Jesus' name we
pray. AMEN.

HYMN: "Now Thank We All Our God" or
      "My God, I Thank Thee"

BENEDICTION:

Dismiss us with thy blessing and may a spirit of thanksgiving
remain with us always. AMEN.

SERVICE 27

ALL ARE BROTHERS
(*United Nations Day*)

A worship center is not always necessary, but if it has meaning, it will contribute to the experience of worship. Helping to prepare a center may be a means of growth in appreciation of worship. A committee of junior highs may be appointed to order the material and prepare the worship center. This will help to establish a feeling of reverence not only in themselves but in others.

An effective center on this day could be made of a large globe of the world surrounded by small flags of various nations set in modeling clay. A flag set and also "The Modern Kit" that tells of the United Nations and how it works may be ordered from the United States Committee for United Nations, 816 21st St., N.W., Washington, D.C.

PRELUDE: Hymn tune "Hymn of Nations"

CALL TO WORSHIP:
  The hour cometh, and now is, when the true worshippers shall worship the Father in spirit and in truth: for the Father seeketh such to worship him.
  God is a Spirit: and they that worship him must worship him in spirit and in truth.[1]

HYMN: "In Christ There Is No East or West" or
  "Let There Be Light, Lord God of Hosts"

RESPONSIVE READING:
Leader: Which commandment is first of all?
Group: And Jesus answered him, . . . thou shalt love the Lord thy
  God with all thy heart, and with all thy soul, and with all thy

mind, and with all thy strength: this is the first commandment.

Leader: And the second is like, namely this, Thou shalt love thy neighbour as thyself. There is none other commandment greater than these. . . .

Group: There is neither Jew nor Greek, there is neither bond nor free, . . . for ye are all one in Christ Jesus. . . .

Leader: Thou wilt keep him in perfect peace, whose mind is stayed on thee: because he trusteth in thee. . . .

Group: And all thy children shall be taught of the Lord; and great shall be the peace of thy children. . . .

Leader: And my people shall dwell in a peaceable habitation, and in sure dwellings, and in quiet resting places.

Group: Peace I leave with you, my peace I give unto you: not as the world giveth, give I unto you.

Leader: Let not your heart be troubled, neither let it be afraid. . . .

Group: They shall not hurt nor destroy in all my holy mountain: for the earth shall be full of the knowledge of the Lord, as the waters cover the sea.[2]

INVOCATION:

Our Father, we come to this worship service seeking to know thy will for our lives. Open our hearts and may we pray sincerely for guidance. Help us to know how to overcome selfish desires and yield ourselves to thy leadership. Forgive our personal and national sins and lead us in paths of peace. We ask it in Jesus' name. AMEN.

LEADER:

Four and one half centuries ago people came from various countries to the shores of America. They brought with them their customs and traditions, and today America is known as a nation of many people.

However, there are some who think of themselves as the only true Americans and often feel superior to others who speak and dress differently. Let us remember that the Indians were the only people living here when the white man came. Our ancestors came from England, France, Spain, Germany, Italy, or some other country.

All these people brought their customs, traditions, ideas, talents, and skill. These gifts from many countries have helped to make America the great nation that it is. Should we think less of some people because their gifts are different from ours?

ALL ARE BROTHERS

George Washington said, "Observe good faith and justice towards all nations; cultivate peace and harmony with all. . . . Give to mankind the . . . example of a people always guided by an exalted justice and benevolence."

Abraham Lincoln said, "With malice toward none; with charity for all; with firmness in the right, as God gives us to see the right, let us strive on to finish the work we are in; . . . to do all which may achieve and cherish a just and lasting peace among ourselves and with all nations."

As we listen to the story "Thirty-two Languages," let us think of our own patriotism and ask ourselves if it is entirely Christian. Let us also think of what needs to be done to make the United Nations strong enough and wise enough to deal adequately with all problems and to bring about a rule of law and justice for all nations of the earth.

STORY:

THIRTY-TWO LANGUAGES

Of course Bob Wright had always heard about the United Nations ever since he could remember. He had studied about it in school back in the U.S.A. Always in October, at Scout meeting, at school, and at church, he had helped celebrate United Nations Day. One year he brought a dime to help buy a United Nations flag for school. Once he had a few lines in a United Nations play for Scouts. One year the junior choir learned a "Song of Peace" to sing in church, but he thought less about the words than about the itchy collar of his junior-choir robe. Of course they said a pledge of allegiance to the United Nations at least once a year at school. Bob had not needed to learn it, because it was always written on the blackboard. He never thought much about the words. When he thought about the United Nations at all, he pictured a lot of little countries that had agreed to "play ball" with his own great country.

All that was when Bob was back home in the United States. Then Bob's family moved to the Middle East, where his father worked with the World Health Organization, the branch of the United Nations that is trying to improve health conditions all over the world. While he sat in the big four-motored plane, zooming along at better than three hundred miles an hour, Bob began to learn what a huge world the United Nations represented.

But it was when he started to school in his new home, in the capital city of a Middle Eastern country, that he really began to think of different nations working together. It was a school for boys and girls whose fathers had come from other lands. Some were working for some branch of the United Nations, such as the Technical Assistance Program or the Food and Agriculture Organization. Some represented their various countries in the embassies and consulates of Pakistan, Switzerland, Denmark, China, Poland. Some were missionaries. Some were technicians from America working with the Foreign Operations Administration, part of the United States' attempt to help other countries.

Luckily for Bob the language of the school was English. The boys and girls from lands with other languages had to do their best with English. With schoolmates able to speak thirty-two different languages, Bob began to get the feel of the idea of the United Nations. He noticed that the best artist in the school was a quiet Armenian boy. The girl who could make them almost hold their breaths as they watched her dance came from Russia. Boys from Holland, Germany, and Turkey were the best players on the volleyball team. Nobody passed his Scouting tests faster than Pavlos from Greece. And Bob's mother kept saying that she had never seen anyone prettier than the girls from India, especially on the days when they wore their bright-colored saris. Bob found to his surprise that being an American did not make him important. With every day that passed, he admired his new friends more and his own self less. In fact, as he saw how good the rest of them were, he was beginning to feel almost too small and unimportant.

Then something happened that made him feel exactly his right size and made him feel that he could take his own part in the little United Nations in which he was living. The school was preparing a Parents' Day Program on the theme "One World." It was to open with a salute to the United Nations flag and a pledge of allegiance spoken in thirty-two different languages. Choosing the ones to speak in some of the languages was easy, because the children speaking those languages were few; but the honor of representing the United States of America might come to any one of a hundred boys and girls.

Every boy and girl in the upper grades knew the teachers were talking it over. When the pupils overheard something like, ". . . has a good voice to be heard outdoors," those with strong voices hoped they were being mentioned. And when they overheard something like, ". . . acts as though living by the pledge," they began to feel sorry about the times they had said mean things about the countries of their schoolmates. Bob kept hoping that the teachers would forget how he acted during his first days of school when he thought that he was important because he was an American.

Finally the announcement came from the principal. "The American to say our United Nations pledge of allegiance will be the boy we feel has learned most in the shortest time about appreciating people of other nations than his own—Bob Wright."

Now Bob knew that he must really learn that pledge of allegiance to the United Nations. He must learn its words and its meaning. He must no longer think of the United Nations as a group of small countries gathered around his own big country. He knew now that the United Nations was made up of many great couutries whose people were like his new school friends. He knew now that only by working with people of these other nations could we have a world that would be always at peace.

That was what Bob tried to put into his voice on the day of the "One World" program. Together the thirty-two of them marched out onto the athletic field and faced their parents in the rows of seats. Together they saluted the United Nations flag of blue and white. Then one by one they gave their pledge of allegiance, each in the language of his own country: "I pledge allegiance to my country and to the United Nations of which it is a part, one world brotherhood of peaceful nations with liberty and justice for all."

Through the program of songs and folk dances of different lands Bob's one-world feeling grew within him. Even if he had been wearing a junior-choir robe with an itchy collar, he would have felt the real meaning of the "Song of Peace," as the whole school and audience together sang it at the close of the program. They sang in English, but they were thinking and feeling in the tongues of thirty-two lands.[3]

POEM:

> I wonder why I cannot see
> The beauty of another's deed;
> And in my soul appreciate
> The truth within another's creed.
>
> Why should I think I have to fight
> A brother with a different name?
> Or why suspect the good intent
> Of him whose faith is not the same?

No church contains the whole of truth,
  No sect the whole of virtue holds,
No human creed contains the whole
  Of all the truths that God unfolds.

And so, today, I bow before
  The Christ of God who meets my need,
For in his life and death I find
  More than the total of all creeds.[4]
—FRED J. JORDAN

PRAYER:

Our Father, we thank thee for our nation and for everything that has helped to make it great. We are grateful for our forefathers who came to these shores to lay the foundation of freedom and brotherhood. Help us to cherish the ideals and to guard the heritage of freedom they passed on to us. Grant that our country may ever be the home of justice, freedom, and brotherhood. To the unfinished task of making our nation a Christian nation, we pledge ourselves to be better followers of thine. To the unfinished task of living as brothers, we also pledge ourselves to strive to practice the golden rule and treat everyone as a brother. Fill our hearts with love and friendliness toward all people. In Jesus' name we pray. AMEN.

HYMN: "O Son of Man, Thou Madest Known" or
      "At Length There Dawns the Glorious Day"

BENEDICTION:

Now unto him who is able to keep us from falling and to present us faultless before the presence of his glory with exceeding joy, to the only wise God be glory now and forever. AMEN.

SERVICE 28

WHO WILL BE FREE?
(Independence Day)

On the Sunday nearest the birthday of our nation we pause for worship. We are rightly proud of the early settlers who came to these shores for religious freedom. We are proud of the handful of men who fought through great difficulty to win the freedom we now enjoy.

The early settlers believed that men are created equal in the sight of God and that they should be free to think for themselves to worship God as their conscience dictates, and to build a democracy. The pioneers to this land had faith in the idea of self-government and were willing to give all that they might govern themselves in peace. Because they acted upon this belief, we live today in a great nation enriched by the heritage of our forefathers.

A picture of the landing of the Pilgrims, or the first Thanksgiving, or Pilgrims going to church would be appropriate in a worship center.

PRELUDE: Hymn tune "National Hymn"

CALL TO WORSHIP:

> God of our fathers . . .
> Thy love divine hath led us in the past;
> In this free land by thee our lot is cast;
> Be thou our Ruler, Guardian, Guide, and Stay;
> Thy word our law, thy paths our chosen way.
> —DANIEL C. ROBERTS

HYMN: "Our God, Our Help in Ages Past" or
"God of Grace and God of Glory"

PRAYER:

Our Father, make us truly thankful for our country, for our fore-fathers who sacrificed to make it free. They gave the last full measure of devotion in order to pass on to us the ideals that have made our country great. Grant that we may never forget what they did and why they did it. Let us not forget the needs of the future while think-ing of the glories of the past. May we not fail our country in its hour of need, but may we see clearly the task ahead of us to bring about a day of peace, brotherhood, and a more abundant life for all people of every country. In Jesus' name we pray. AMEN.

LEADER:

As Independence Day draws near, let us thank God for the free-dom that has come to us, for our forefathers who believed that all men are created equal and should have certain rights.

FROM THE DECLARATION OF INDEPENDENCE:

We hold these truths to be self-evident,—that all men are created equal; that they are endowed by their Creator with certain unalienable rights; that among these are life, liberty, and the pursuit of happiness.

"Those who deny freedom to others deserve it not for themselves."—

ABRAHAM LINCOLN.

"No one can be perfectly free till all are free."—HERBERT SPENCER.

"For every man who lives without freedom the rest of us must face the guilt."—LILLIAN HELLMAN.

FROM THE SCRIPTURES:

Proclaim liberty throughout all the land unto all the inhabitants thereof. . . .

Where the spirit of the Lord is, there is liberty. . . .

Therefore all things whatsoever ye would that men should do to you, do ye even so to them: for this is the law and the prophets.[1]

LEADER:

We will hear the story of the statue of liberty. The lady with the torch is a symbol of the freedoms for which our country has fought and that she offers to people coming to our shores.

Story:

BARTHOLDI'S MOTHER

"Liberty! Equality! Fraternity!" are three words that the boy Auguste learned from his tall and handsome mother, Charlotte Bartholdi. He learned more than the sound of them or the feel of them on his tongue. He learned what they meant to the people in France in the middle of the last century. Liberty—that everyone in France should be free to think, to speak, and to live his best. Equality—that no man in France was better than another, whether he lived in a tiny hut or a nobleman's palace. Fraternity—that all people of France were brothers.

The boy Auguste loved to listen to his mother's stories of their ancestor General Beysser, a hero of the French Revolution. There was something special in the way she held her head when she told what General Beysser had done to bring freedom to France. As Auguste grew older, he always connected his tall and handsome mother with liberty, equality, and fraternity.

He left the home with its gables, covered balconies, and spire. But he never forgot what his mother had taught him. He grew up to be a sculptor, but he was never satisfied with a statue that was only beautiful. His statues must have a meaning.

Once he was hired to make a statue of a teacher, Édouard de Laboulaye. While Bartholdi was at the De Laboulaye home in the summer of 1865, some guests were invited for dinner. They talked about liberty, equality, and fraternity. The sculptor liked to hear again the ideas and the words that were so dear to his own mother.

Édouard de Laboulaye was a Frenchman who felt that France and America were sister countries that would always work for liberty, equality, and fraternity. At that time the people in America were thinking of freedom for Negro slaves, and the people of France were thinking of freedom from neighboring nations, that were threatening to invade their country. That, as De Laboulaye told the friends gathered in his home, made France and America closer sisters than ever.

"Remember how Lafayette helped when America was fighting for its freedom," he said to his friends. "Remember how America's freedom gave France courage to win its own. If a monument should be built in the United States as a memorial to their independence, it should be built by united effort, a common work of both nations."

The word "monument" caught the ears of the young sculptor. A monument representing the liberty that was France and the liberty that was America! What a dream for the son of Charlotte Bartholdi!

While Auguste Bartholdi talked with the people of France about a statue, he wondered how he would represent liberty in bronze or in stone. Édouard de Laboulaye and others liked the idea of the statue and started raising money for its making. It would be the perfect gift from France to celebrate the one hundredth birthday of the United States in 1876. Because the Americans must raise money to build the pedestal, it would become "the common work of both nations."

But how could Auguste Bartholdi tell the story of liberty by a statue? He thought of great men who had worked for liberty—George Washington or Lafayette. But other sculptors had made statues of them. As he went about his other work, there was always the question in the back of his mind—how to create a statue that would make all men think of freedom. He talked it over with his mother, who had taught him to love liberty, equality, and fraternity. Even Charlotte Bartholdi could not suggest a symbol that would stand for the liberty of France and the liberty of America.

Finally the time came for Bartholdi to make his first trip to the United States to talk with Americans about the statue. Still he did not know what symbol to use for liberty. During the voyage across the ocean he was wondering how he could describe the monument to Americans. He had no answers to the questions they would surely ask:

"Where will the statue be located?"

"How will it look?"

"What use will it be?"

The night before the ship was due to dock in New York harbor, he went to bed with not an idea worth giving to the committee he was to meet the next day. A sculptor should have a small model of the statue he plans to make—at least a sketch of it. He had nothing to show.

He woke early the next morning and looked through his porthole. Land was near. He dressed quickly and went on deck. He gazed ahead at something he had never seen before—the skyline of New York City. In those days it was not the skyline of towering buildings we see today. Then, no building was higher than the steeple of Trinity Church. Even so, it was a skyline of beauty—church spires, city buildings, homes spreading out into the country. And all about him ships were going and coming in the busy rivers and bays of New York. He felt the strength and power of a land that was free.

Suddenly his idea came to him. Taking a pencil, he quickly sketched the outline of New York Harbor. Then he pictured from an island in the bay a mighty woman rising with a high-held torch in one hand

and something that might have been a big book of laws under her other arm. She was a tall and handsome woman who held her head high, certain that all was well in a world where liberty, equality, and fraternity ruled. Auguste Bartholdi did not have to wonder how the woman of his statue should look. He knew.

Probably you have heard most of the story of the years of work that stretched between Bartholdi's quick sketch of the statue of Liberty Enlightening the World and the day in 1886 when the statue was dedicated on Bedloe's Island in New York Harbor.

There is one part of the story that is seldom told. On the day when the model of the Statue of Liberty was unveiled in France, Auguste Bartholdi was showered with praise for his work. But he knew who should share credit with him. That evening he invited a friend to go with him to the theater.

"I have a special reason for asking you to come," Bartholdi told his friend.

As Bartholdi and his guest walked into the box, they saw a tall and handsome woman sitting in the corner seat in the front of the box. The guest gasped at sight of her.

"She is the statue," he whispered, "Liberty Enlightening the World!"

"Yes, she is," answered the sculptor. "May I present you to Madame Charlotte Bartholdi—my mother."

Since 1886 the Statue of Liberty has meant the freedom of America to the millions of persons who have sailed in and out of New York Harbor, and to the millions more who have looked at it from shore. Even those who have never been to New York City know by her picture the tall woman holding up her torch to enlighten the world. But very few know they are looking at the statue of Charlotte Bartholdi, a French mother who taught her son to love liberty, equality, and fraternity. Liberty—that everyone in the world should be free to think, to speak, and to live his best. Equality—that a man is a man whether he lives in a tiny hut or a rich man's palace. Fraternity—that all men everywhere are brothers.[2]

LEADER:

As we think of the risks our forefathers took to be free, let us remember there is much left for us to do to keep our country free.

Can a country remain free when there are people within its borders enslaved by fear and hatred? Can it be great when there are forces that divide and weaken it? What can be done to get rid of prejudice among races, poverty and hunger? How can all people learn to work for the common good of all?

Freedom does not just happen today any more than it just happened in 1776. Independence Day is a time for all of us to renew our pledge to protect a heritage handed down to us over 180 years ago.

POEM:

>Lord, while for all mankind we pray,
>   Of every clime and coast,
>O hear us for our native land,
>   The land we love the most.
>
>O guard our shores from every foe;
>   With peace our borders bless;
>With prosp'rous times our cities crown,
>   Our fields with plenteousness.
>
>Unite us in the sacred love
>   Of knowledge, truth, and thee;
>And let our hills and valleys shout
>   The songs of liberty.
>   —JOHN R. WREFORD

LEADER:

As we sing this hymn written by Chauncey R. Piety, let us think of the words. The author gives thanks to God for our country, for life and liberty, for justice and good will, and also for the glory that shall come in the future.

HYMN: "THANKS, THANKS TO GOD"
(Tune "National Hymn," "God of Our Fathers, Whose Almighty Hand")

>Thanks, thanks to God for lovely native land,
>Thanks that our homes and schools and churches stand,
>Thanks for our cities, farms, and halls of state,
>Thanks for our laws and people good and great.
>
>Thanks, thanks to God for life and liberty,
>Thanks for the great achievements of the free,
>Thanks for inventions, science, music, art,
>Thanks for high aims and hopes that hold each heart.

174

WHO WILL BE FREE?

Thanks, thanks to God for justice and good will,
Thanks for the works our God is working still,
Thanks for the good in human history,
Thanks to our God for glory that shall be.[3]

—CHAUNCEY R. PIETY

PRAYER:

Our Father, we thank thee for the early pioneers who settled our country, built homes in the wilderness, and founded our nation. We are grateful for the churches, schools, and libraries that they built and for the heritage passed on to us. Help us not only to keep the laws of our country, but to be true to the ideals upon which the nation was founded. Grant that we may not depend too much upon armies and material power, but may we cherish and live by the truths that guided our forefathers. Help us to uproot false pride, racial prejudice, oppression, injustice, or anything that tends to divide the people. Fill our hearts with love for thee and with sympathy and understanding for all people. In Jesus' name we pray. AMEN.

HYMN: "O God, Beneath Thy Guiding Hand" or
"God Save America"

BENEDICTION:

Dismiss us with thy blessing and help us to be willing to share with others coming to our shores the blessings that we have received. AMEN.

SERVICE 29

PUTTING FIRST THINGS FIRST
(*Decision Day*)

Among the early Christians there were those who started to follow Jesus without counting the cost. They may have had wrong ambitions or mistaken ideas about what to expect. Jesus said to them, "If any man would come after me, let him deny himself, and take up his cross daily, and follow me. For whosoever will save his life shall lose it: but whosoever will lose his life for my sake, the same shall save it." (Luke 9:23-24.)

On one occasion a young man came to Jesus inquiring what to do to inherit eternal life. When Jesus asked about his life, the rich young ruler replied that he had kept all the commandments. The Master suggested that he go sell his goods, give to the poor, and then come and follow him. The young man went away sorrowful, for he was not willing to share his possessions and lose himself in a cause big enough to demand his best.

There are teen-agers who will keep the rules of society but will miss their chance of following Jesus because they will not lose themselves in the cause of Jesus. There are stumbling blocks in the way of those who set out to be followers. Some begin with high resolves but miss the way because they are too easily influenced by the crowd. There are others who lack steadfastness; they follow when things are easy, but when they must face hardship, they become discouraged. Others miss their chance because following Jesus is not the safest or the most popular thing to do.

When teen-agers follow Jesus, it is often necessary to take risks. At times it is necessary to go against their group. In order to choose right, they need to examine their lives in the light of the example of Jesus. They need frequently to call upon God for strength and courage to meet the demands made upon them and to live by the highest and best they know.

PRELUDE: Hymn tune "Consolation"

176

PUTTING FIRST THINGS FIRST

CALL TO WORSHIP:

I will lift up mine eyes unto the hills, from whence
cometh my help.
My help cometh from the Lord, which made heaven
and earth.[1]

INVOCATION:

O God, grant that in this service we may be conscious of thy presence. Speak to us and show us what thou wouldst have us to do. Guide our thoughts and actions that we may be instruments of thine. Use us in helping to build thy kingdom on earth. In Jesus' name. AMEN.

RESPONSIVE READING:

Leader: With my whole heart have I sought thee:
O let me not wander from thy commandments.
Group: Take thou our minds, dear Lord, we humbly pray;
Give us the mind of Christ each passing day;
Teach us to know the truth that sets us free;
Grant us in all our thoughts to honor thee.
Leader: Teach me thy way, O Lord; I will walk in thy truth:
Unite my heart to fear thy name.
Group: Take thou our hearts, O Christ, they are thine own;
Come thou within our souls and claim thy throne;
Help us to shed abroad thy deathless love;
Use us to make the earth like heaven above.
Leader: Teach me thy statutes.
Make me to understand the way of thy precepts:
So shall I talk of thy wondrous works.
Group: Take thou our wills, Most High! Hold thou full sway;
Have in our inmost souls thy perfect way;
Guard thou each sacred hour from selfish ease;
Guide thou our ordered lives as thou dost please.
Leader: Let the words of my mouth, and the meditation of
my heart, be acceptable in thy sight,
O Lord, my strength, and my redeemer.[2]
Group: Take thou ourselves, O Lord, heart, mind, and will;
Through our surrendered souls thy plans fulfill.
We yield ourselves to thee—time, talents, all;
We hear, and henceforth heed, thy sovereign call.

—AUTHOR UNKNOWN

HYMN: "Master, Touch Us" or
"I Bind My Heart This Tide"

POEM:

> O Jesus, Prince of life and truth,
>   Beneath thy banner bright,
> We dedicate our strength and youth
>   To battle for the right;
> We give our lives with glad intent
>   To serve the world and thee,
> To die, to suffer and be spent,
>   To set our brothers free.
>
> . . . .
>
> O Jesus once a Nazareth boy,
>   And tempted like as we,
> All inward foes help us destroy,
>   And spotless all to be.
> We trust thee for the grace to win
>   The high, victorious goal,
> Where purity shall conquer sin
>   In Christlike self-control.
>
> —AUTHOR UNKNOWN

LEADER:
We will hear the story of the calling of one of the disciples.

STORY:

THE TWO SEARCHERS

Peter was tired of doing the same thing over and over and he wanted a change. Ever since he could remember he had fished and sold the fish he had caught. He had made nets and mended them. First he had done it for his father, and now he owned the boats and nets and fishing implements. But he stood on that bright summer day close by the beautiful lake of Gennesaret in Galilee, wishing over and over that he could do something that was more worth while.

There was a reason why Peter was more discouraged than ever on this morning. He had fished all through the night before in the hope of getting a good catch so that he might skip a day's work and go to hear the great teacher about whom men were talking and whom Andrew, his brother, had seen. But though he had worked hard, not a fish had he caught. So now he was mending the holes in the net with a very discontented look on his face. What was the use of it all, anyway? He twisted the rope this way and that, showing by the pulls that he made that his mind was full of trouble.

Suddenly he heard Andrew talking to him. "Peter," he said, "Peter, see the crowd coming over the hilltop. Perhaps the teacher is coming. I do hope so, for I would hear more of the words he was telling us yesterday. Come, let's go and meet him."

"No," said Peter, "I must finish this net. What will he care for us? We are only poor fishermen."

But Andrew had not waited to hear his answer—he had already begun to ascend the hill. How eager he was to hear another story from the great story-teller!

Peter mended one hole after another, keeping his eye on the crowd that was coming closer and closer to the lakeside. Then he heard a kindly voice say, "Would you mind letting me take your boat, for the multitude press upon me and I have many things to say to them. If I can get away from the shore, they can all hear and understand."

Silently Peter brought the fishing boat to shore. The Master wanted to use something that he had. After all, a fishing boat was useful sometimes, even if he were tired of it. Of course he would be glad to help Him. So Jesus, the teacher, sat in the end of the boat and Peter rowed Him out in front of the crowd. Then Peter sat and listened and looked.

What a wonderful face the teacher had! Peter had never seen the like. It was browned by the sun but in the eyes there was a kindly light that made Peter love to look at Him. When He smiled, somehow Peter felt the smile go all through him. How gentle His voice was! What made it so? How eagerly the people were listening, yet He was only telling them a little story about the love of His father, God.

"I wish I had a face like that and a voice like that and could teach like that," thought Peter. "But I am only a poor fisherman. Oh dear, I wish I could be worth something."

But Jesus had finished teaching and had bidden the people to go to their homes. Peter turned to row to the shore, but Jesus was not ready for that. He had been teaching the multitude and now He wanted a chance to talk with Peter and Andrew. So He said to Peter, "Launch out into the deep and let us fish for a while."

Peter thought of the long night of useless toil, but Jesus had asked him to go. This was a chance to stay longer with the teacher, so he said to him frankly, "Master, we have toiled all night and caught nothing. Nevertheless, at your word, I will let down the net."

So together the brothers let down the net and Peter began to row. This was a good chance for Jesus to study Peter. How strong and weatherbeaten he looked! His was a good honest face, and Jesus saw there determination and courage and trustworthiness. Jesus was searching for men who could be trusted to carry in their minds and lives the most precious thing He had—His message to the world—so as He rowed out into the fishing grounds of Lake Gennesaret that day, He was searching Peter's face. It would take courage, for some of His followers would even have to die for Him. It would take determination, for there would be many things against them. Yes, Jesus liked Peter as He watched him and talked to him. Peter was one of the men for whom He was searching.

Suddenly the net was full of fishes—so full that Peter and Andrew could not manage it. Quickly they called to their partners, James and John, to come and help them. And when Peter saw the multitude of fishes that were in the net, he was overpowered with the greatness of the man who had helped them. Quickly he fell on his knees before the Christ and said, "Depart from me, O Lord, for I am a sinful man."

Then Jesus turned to Peter and with a whole world of meaning said, "Peter, it is a great multitude of fishes that you have caught, but you can do greater things than that. You can do far greater things than catch fish from the water. If you will come with me, I will teach you how to catch men and you shall be my worker. I need you, Peter. Will you come?"

Would he come? Peter, who had been longing to make his life worth while; Peter, who had been longing to know what it was that made Jesus so wonderful as He went among men. Would he go and let Jesus teach him? Would he be a follower of the Master and go out in the big world to help win men?

A great happiness filled the mind of Peter and when he lifted his face to the Christ, the answer to the question of the Teacher was written on it.[3]

Scripture:

And Jesus, walking by the sea of Galilee, saw two brethren, Simon called Peter, and Andrew his brother, casting a net into the sea: for they were fishers. And he saith unto them, Follow me, and I will make you fishers of men. And they straightway left their nets, and followed him.[4]

POEM:

>O Master, who in the days of youth
>Didst walk the path of light and truth,
>Keep thou our feet upon the way
>That leads to everlasting day.
>
>Help us in days of youth to see
>Visions of what our lives may be;
>One fellowship in Christ our aim,
>Our joy to magnify thy name.
>
>O thou, who from thy youth didst prove
>The highest law of life is love,
>Fill thou our hearts with love divine,
>And through our lives forever shine.[5]
>—H. GLEN LANIER

PRAYER:

O Master of our lives, help us to make the decision to follow thee. As we think of thee may it not be merely the memory of a life lived long ago, but a spirit living within us today. May thy life challenge all that is mean and low within us and help us to reach out to better living. May a measure of thy love be seen in our thoughts, attitudes, and action. Help us to uproot selfishness and center our thoughts on what we can do for others. Help us to get a vision of the strength and beauty of thy life. In spite of our weaknesses and shortcomings we offer our lives to thee. May thy spirit be with us as we try to win others to thee and help to bring in thy kingdom. In thy name we pray. AMEN.

HYMN: "Just As I Am, Thine Own to Be" or
   "Take My Life and Let It Be"

BENEDICTION:

Dismiss us with thy blessing and grant us a sense of thy presence in the days ahead. AMEN.

SERVICE 30

HE IS RISEN
(*Easter*)

The Lenten period is a good time for junior highs to learn the meaning of Christ in one's life. Through worship they may discover that when Christ comes into one's life, choices should be made according to Christian ways of living. Those who are beginning to follow Christ may need help in working out their own standards of conduct. This is not easy, for it often means going against one's group to keep these standards. Others who are already followers of Christ may dedicate themselves anew to God's will for their lives. The entire group will need strength and courage to live up to their good resolutions. Inspiration and encouragement come as they learn more about Christ and his way of life.

A good Easter picture would be appropriate as a center of worship. A. H. Ender, "The Holy Women at the Tomb," may be ordered from your denominational supply house or from Wilde Religious Pictures, 131 Clarendon St., Boston 16, Massachusetts. If a suitable picture is not available, a cross flanked with lighted candles would be effective. Sometimes it is possible to borrow pictures from a public library.

PRELUDE: "Religioso" by Chopin

CALL TO WORSHIP:
Surely he hath borne our griefs, and carried our sorrows: yet we did esteem him stricken, smitten of God, and afflicted.

But he was wounded for our transgressions, he was bruised for our iniquities: the chastisement of our peace was upon him; and with his stripes we are healed.[1]

HYMN: "Come, Ye Faithful, Raise the Strain" or
"The Day of Resurrection"

182

HE IS RISEN

PRAYER:

Our Father, we seek thy presence, asking for guidance in the problems that we face from day to day. Help each one of us to accept the crosses that come to us and with thy help conquer them and become better Christians. Show us what is right and may we choose the best in day by day living. In Jesus' name we pray. AMEN.

SCRIPTURE:

In the end of the sabbath, as it began to dawn toward the first day of the week, came Mary Magdalene and the other Mary to see the sepulchre. And, behold, there was a great earthquake: for the angel of the Lord descended from heaven, and came and rolled back the stone from the door, and sat upon it. His countenance was like lightning, and his raiment white as snow: and for fear of him the keepers did shake, and became as dead men. And the angel answered and said unto the women, Fear not ye: for I know that ye seek Jesus, which was crucified. He is not here: for he is risen, as he said. Come, see the place where the Lord lay. And go quickly, and tell his disciples that he is risen from the dead; and behold, he goeth before you into Galilee; there shall ye see him: lo, I have told you. And they departed quickly from the sepulchre with fear and great joy; and did run to bring his disciples word.[2]

POEM:

Christ is arisen.
  Joy to thee, mortal!
Out of his prison,
  Forth from its portal!
Christ is not sleeping,
  Seek him no longer;
Strong was his keeping,
  Jesus was stronger.

Christ is arisen.
  Seek him not here;
Lonely his prison,
  Empty his bier;
Vain his entombing,
  Spices and lawn,
Vain the perfuming,
  Jesus is gone.

183

Christ is arisen.
  Joy to thee, mortal!
Empty his prison,
  Broken its portal!
Rising, he giveth
  His shroud to the sod;
Risen, he liveth,
  And liveth to God.
—JOHANN WOLFGANG VON GOETHE
  TR. A. C. COXE

STORY:

WHEN PILATE HEARD THE NEWS

It had been a bad day for Pontius Pilate, governor of Jerusalem. Those hotheaded Jews, always a difficult people to rule, had been more than ordinarily restless and troublesome of late. Nothing that a governor could do seemed to please them. Great festivals, such as those provided for the populace by Caesar back in Rome, were held in fine contempt by these fanatics. Gladiatorial combats, so popular among the Romans, were simply out of the question with these people. Entertainments and public buildings, eminently satisfactory elsewhere in the empire, seemed only to widen the breach between the government and the people. To make matters worse, there had been an epidemic of banditry and rebellion in Palestine ever since Pilate had arrived to take charge of the province.

One of the most difficult situations of all had arisen just two days ago. A young carpenter had stirred up the Jewish leaders to a frenzy over some silly religious matter. On nothing were the Jews more touchy than on matters of religion, and this man had offended the priests and teachers with his revolutionary ideas.

This young carpenter had taken matters into his own hands a few days earlier and created a scene in the temple over the selling of sheep and pigeons inside the sacred precincts. As a matter of fact, everybody had known about the graft connected with the business for a long time, but most people had come to accept it as a matter of course. Some rather important people had an interest in the system, and the young man's surprise attack had thoroughly aroused the business interests of the community. The result was that the priests and dignitaries of the Jews came into Pilate's court, clamoring and threatening and demanding that the young carpenter be executed.

Pilate had gone into the matter rather perfunctorily and in all probability would have dismissed the case, but the Jews made an extremely uncomfortable issue out of it by charging the carpenter with treason. "He calls himself a king," they reported, and this naturally had to be investigated.

The governor was much inclined to befriend the young man, for he had heard about him from his own wife, Claudia. She reported that he was a man of strange and winsome power, who seemed able to answer the deep questions that eager souls kept asking. Claudia, of course, was a woman, and women are expected to be a bit emotional.

Still, Pilate had secretly wished he might ask the young man a few questions himself. There were some strange stirrings in his own heart that the Roman philosophers had never been able to explain. When the young man came before him for trial, however, he had been quite noncommittal, as if he did not think he would be understood, even if he did talk.

There was one remark he had dropped, though, that Pilate had not been able to forget. "My kingdom is a kingdom of truth," the carpenter had said. Somehow that remark would not down. Pilate had been thinking about it ever since. A thousand times—even sometimes in the midst of a difficult case—he had found himself thinking about the young man, his remarkable face, and that cryptic remark. And always he returned to the same question, "What is truth?"

Even at the time it had not seemed like a very just decision, but the Jews were so clamorous and threatening, and the young man had seemed to be of no particular importance, that Pilate, in spite of a solemn warning from his wife, had finally issued an order for his execution. Life under Rome was always cheap, and it seemed better for one man to die than for the entire city to be plunged into an uproar. But from the time the carpenter disappeared through the doors of the judgment hall and was led off to Calvary for crucifixion, Pilate had not been able to get him off his mind.

The day of the crucifixion had seemed a day of weird fates. Suddenly, in the midst of the afternoon, a deep darkness had mysteriously spread over the city, plunging it into inky blackness. The earth had shaken until buildings reeled and tottered like drunken men. Panic reigned throughout the city.

A young priest, hurrying over from the high priest's house, had brought a message imploring a double guard over the grave of the young carpenter, for, said he, "It is said that this man has promised that he will rise from the grave after three days, and we do not want his disciples stealing his body and pretending a resurrection."

Though Pilate had no patience with the Jews' religion, he was smart enough to sense what it would mean to the city to have any such rumor circulated. It seemed that this youth would not be dismissed, even by death! A guard therefore was placed at the tomb, and the governor's seal affixed to the stone before the entrance of the tomb.

And now, two days later, the governor was returning from his court. His step was that of a man tired beyond endurance. The day had not been so different from other days, but the load on his mind was becoming unendurable. "What is truth? What is truth?" He had asked the question over and over.

Suddenly an excited courier came hurriedly down the corridor. "My Lord," he gasped breathlessly in a frantic effort to appear calm, *"he is alive!"*

Pilate's heart stood still. Speech for a second seemed an impossibility. Then, summoning a calm he could only pretend, he asked, "Who is alive?" But his voice trembled in spite of himself. He knew before he was answered.

"The Galilean!" the courier shouted, all pretense at control now gone. "The town is full of the word. The women have seen him. His disciples have seen him. The tomb is empty. *He is risen!"*

Without a word Pilate turned and staggered to his room. His brain kept telling him there must be some mistake, but in his heart he knew it was true. The young man was alive! Truth does not die! He had stood face to face with truth and had not known it!

It was hours afterward when Claudia came upon him, staring out into the night. His face was drawn and white. His lips moved falteringly, but no words issued from them. He seemed oblivious to all the world about him. He was as a man who has read the writing of his own doom.

The sound of Claudia's step upon the stone seemed to penetrate to his benumbed brain, and he turned upon her as a man would turn in his grave. "Have you heard?" the woman asked, scarcely speaking.

Pilate only nodded. He stared at Claudia as if she might have been a visitor from another planet. For seconds—seconds that seemed eternities—they stood thus. At last he spoke, and his words fell, clattering like hail upon the cobblestones. "He is risen. He is truth! *I crucified God!"* [3]

Poem:

> This is the beauty of our Easter morning:
> In him humanity may now arise

HE IS RISEN

Out of the grave of self, all baseness scorning—
  The holy radiance of his glorious eyes
Illumines everywhere uplifted faces;
  Touches the earthly with a heavenly glow;
All in that blessed light all human graces
  Unto divine beatitudes must grow.

—LUCY LARCOM

PRAYER:

O God, we are grateful for the first Easter, for the hope that Easter brings. We are grateful that thou hast promised eternal life to those who believe and follow thee. Help us to begin living here the kind of life that is worthy to endure. Help us to become sensitive to the needs of others. May we walk each day in the way of love and helpfulness, showing kindness and consideration to all and treating all men as brothers. May we follow the example of Jesus by striving to find and follow thy will for our lives. Teach us thy ways, and we will walk in thy paths. In Jesus' name. AMEN.

HYMN: "Christ the Lord Is Risen Today" or
      "Crown Him with Many Crowns"

BENEDICTION:

Dismiss us in thy favor and may we walk in newness of life in the days that are ahead. AMEN.

SERVICE 31

CHRIST LIVES TODAY
(*Easter*)

PRELUDE: "I Know That My Redeemer Liveth" (*Messiah*) by Handel

CALL TO WORSHIP:
> To this end Christ both died, and rose, and revived,
> That he might be Lord both of the dead and living. . . .
> Sing unto the Lord a new song, and his praise from
>   the end of the earth.[1]

LEADER:

Easter is a time for praise, and song is the language of praise. Let us think of the happiness of the disciples when they learned that Jesus was alive. In Easter hymns that joy is expressed of the triumph of Jesus over death and of light over darkness.

HYMN: "Sing with All the Sons of Glory" or
> "When I Survey the Wondrous Cross" or
> " 'Mid All the Traffic of the Ways"

INVOCATION:

O Lord, we come with joy because thou hast overcome death and brought light to all people. Help us better to understand the meaning of Easter and strengthen our determination to live more like thee. AMEN.

SCRIPTURE:

Now when the centurion, and they that were with him, watching Jesus, saw the earthquake, and those things that were done, they feared greatly, saying, Truly this was the Son of God. . . .

188

CHRIST LIVES TODAY

Now the next day, ... the chief priests and Pharisees came together unto Pilate,

Saying, Sir, we remember that that deceiver said, while he was yet alive, After three days I will rise again.

Command therefore that the sepulchre be made sure until the third day, lest his disciples come by night, and steal him away, and say unto the people, He is risen from the dead: so the last error shall be worse than the first.

Pilate said unto them, Ye have a watch: go your way, make it as sure as you can.

So they went, and made the sepulchre sure, sealing the stone, and setting a watch. . . .

Now when they were going, behold, some of the watch came into the city, and shewed unto the chief priests all the things that were done.

And when they were assembled with the elders, and had taken counsel, they gave large money unto the soldiers,

Saying, Say ye, His disciples came by night, and stole him away while we slept. . . .

So they took the money, and did as they were taught.[2]

LEADER:

We will hear the story of one of the soldiers whose task it was to guard the tomb in which Jesus was laid.

STORY:

THE BLOND SOLDIER

The three men had reached into their rich garments, produced several small but full moneybags, and tossed them lightly on the table.

The soldiers stared at them, somewhat incredulous.

"Looks like a small fortune," observed the petty officer in charge. "Is it ours? Easy money, I hope. My lords, tell us exactly what we have to do for it."

"Nothing, my friend."

"Nothing—do you say?"

"Nothing—except to keep your tongues locked in your heads."

The petty officer seemed to understand. He glanced at his soldiers, then gazed hard at the three men.

"But—what if we're questioned?"

"Then say that His disciples came by night and stole His body out of the grave."

There was a halting pause. For a moment nothing was said.

"That," declared one of the soldiers abruptly, "is a lie! We all saw what happened."

The other soldiers turned to look at him, startled. The three men—elders, dignified officials from the court of Caiaphas and strangely out of place in this common tavern—glared with sudden contempt. But the soldier met all eyes steadily. He was young, very blond-haired, husky of body, and he seemed completely unafraid.

"What do you, a northern barbarian, know of telling the truth?" sneered the petty officer, his immediate superior.

The blond soldier cracked a faint smile.

"Pilate," he said boldly, "will be more careful with his crucifixions hereafter—and we know it."

That halting silence fell again. All the soldiers squirmed a little. The three dignitaries from the high priest's court noticed it and frowned darkly.

Then the petty officer seemed to rouse himself, laughing and frowning almost at the same time. "As I told you, he's just a barbarian," he tried to explain, inclining his head toward the blond soldier. "Look at his yellow hair. A young German from the Teutoburg Woods—a savage who studies, asks questions, and nurses strange ideas in his head. And besides all this, he's in love—romantic about some slave girl, of all people—"

Instantly the blond soldier sprang to his feet. His blue eyes glittered dangerously. "Leave the girl out of this—"

"Sit down, youngster!" growled his superior with a menacing stare, "and close that free mouth of yours before its gets you into real trouble. Nobody will force money on you—if you want to be a fool!"

"Not a fool," returned the blond one, "only fair."

Now it appeared that the three men from the Sanhedrin had enough of this totally unexpected opposition. One, a portly gray-bearded Pharisee, addressed himself to the blond soldier.

"Look," he said smoothly, "you are only a boy. What do you know? You will listen to men older than you, and you will change your mind."

The blond soldier rose to face him.

"You look!" he told him sharply. "I may be a boy, and a barbarian from the woods, but, thanks to Caesar's legions, I get around and keep my eyes open—and my head, too. You tell me—how could I change my mind? This is a rotten world, thick with the dirt of hate, greed, and deceit. Bloody, too. Many will cut throats for money, power, and glory. This Jesus of Nazareth, He was none of that; He was good—and we nailed Him to the cross. For what?"

"Who knows?" mocked the Pharisee, his black eyes narrowing to slits. "Do you know?"

The blond soldier raised his head.

"Yes," he said. "I know. I believe what He said. He came to plant good in this rotten world and save it from evil, and many don't want that, so they slew Him!"

"Ah!" snapped the Pharisee. "Did your slave girl sweetheart tell you that?"

This time the blond solider kept calm. Levelly he answered: "He said to Himself—many times, lately to the High Priest and to the Governor. You heard it. But yes—and she said it, too. My little slave girl sweetheart, as you call her, has more wisdom than many rabbis, all put together. Yes, she said it! And so did our Roman captain at the cross, and others. You know that the man who betrayed Him hanged himself because he saw his own mountainous guilt. Now I'll say it, too. He isn't of this world. He came from beyond the earth, where He has His Kingdom. You Hebrews talk of God. He is the *Son* of God, a *King,* just as He said, and only through *Him* can any of us human creatures ever see God!"

The silence that followed this seemed tremendous. The three men from the Sanhedrin looked outraged, furious.

"You believe, then, that He arose alive from the grave?" challenged the gray-bearded Pharisee in a tense, deadly voice.

"Don't you?" returned the blond soldier. "We do. We saw it, only this morning."

Nobody knew what to say. The blond soldier turned and pointed to his companions.

"Ask them. They all saw. They're still scared cold and stiff by what they saw. Something not of our earth, not of weak men—but something almighty, a wonder of supernatural power and glory. They will never forget it. Oh, they might take your money, but they'll know the truth."

Again that deadly silence. The soldiers seemed definitely uneasy. The three men from the Sanhedrin appeared to grow angrier by the minute. Suddenly the petty officer's fist came down on the table with a bang.

"Enough of this!" he snapped. "Who cares about rabbis and God and supernatural glory? I'm a Roman. What is truth? My lords, what you ask shall be done. Depend on it."

"And what of this—young radical here?" demanded the Pharisee, pointing his finger straight at the blond soldier.

"He'll know enough to keep his mouth shut, or we'll slap him in a deep, dark, silent dungeon," promised the officer grimly.

That was the end of the meeting. The money changed hands, and the biggest campaign of falsehood in the history of the world had begun.

Soon after, the blond soldier walked alone through the early evening toward a certain place at the foot of Mount Olivet. A fine country house stood there. The blond Roman legionary went around to the rear and rattled softly at an iron wicket in the wall. In a moment the slave girl appeared, dressed in a poor garment but looking young and pretty. She gazed at the blond soldier with complete love in her eyes. Together they sat down to talk and watch the quiet red sunset that was spreading above the hills.

He seemed very deep in thought.

"Do you know what has happened now?" he burst out suddenly.

"Something—important?" she asked.

"Yes. Something that never in this world will stop being important. They are trying to hush the truth."

"Who?"

"Men from Caiaphas' court. Powerful, rich politicians. Pious, smooth, talking of God, but thinking of their own interests, first and only. Hard as glass inside. They still hate Him! He interfered with their business and their whole life. He showed them their heart. He taught love; they want power. But how can men hate Him who came to love and save them and everyone else? Tell me that, my sweet."

The girl shook her head. "I don't know," she murmured. "All I know is that I love Him. And you! We know He is alive!"

"I should know, *carissima!* I was there!" He took her hand. "This open grave," he said softly, "this is the living proof for all He said! Don't you see?"

She nodded wonderingly. "He died—and He lives again! Only God could do it!"

"Right. God. This living Jesus is God—and for all of us! Think of that, my love. For every human being on earth. To Him you are not a slave, I am not a barbarian mercenary—we are the children of a King! We can live and die and live again—just as He. Immortality—

a fact!" The blond soldier laughed and put his arm tenderly around her. "You and I," he told her happily, "we can live forever!"

She looked at him with lovely, misty eyes. But his own eyes were serious.

"And this," he said, "is the truth they're trying to keep from the world! Let them try! Let them try—now in that scheming court of Caiaphas and in all ages to come! They will always fail, my loved one! Always—like that sunset there, like the solid earth itself, like the stars and seas and mountains—always, no matter what men may say or do—the truth will be the truth!"

So they sat there—two young people facing life over nineteen hundred years ago, happy and certain of heart, watching the wonder and glory of the first Easter Day.[3]

PRAYER:

Our Father, we are grateful for the triumph of Christ over death, for the hope that Easter brings. Help us better to understand the meaning of this day. May we realize that because Christ lives, we, too, may live in newness of life. Teach us and guide us into the meaning of the Christian life; take away our doubts; give us strength to live at our best every day and courage to do right even when the crowd is against us. Forgive our mistakes and weaknesses and help us to be better followers of thine. In Jesus' name. AMEN.

HYMN: "All Glory, Laud, and Honor" or
"All Hail the Power of Jesus' Name"

BENEDICTION:

Dismiss us with thy blessing and may we live as sons and daughters of thine in the days that are ahead. AMEN.

SERVICE 32

WISE MEN BRING THEIR GIFTS
(Christmas)

The Advent Season is a good time to strengthen the faith of teen-agers. The leaders should be selected carefully and allowed sufficient time to prepare the material. Their manner should be reverent and sincere in the presentation. The lighting of candles and singing of Christmas carols will give deeper meaning to Christmas. It could be explained that a lighted candle is a symbol of the light and joy that the coming of Jesus brought to the world.

For use in the worship center select the best that is available of Nativity pictures. In the service "Wise Men Bring Their Gifts" use Sassetta, "The Journey of the Wise Men"; or Fra Filippo Lippi and Fra Angelico, "The Adoraof the Magi." For the service "Christmas for Everyone" use Correggio, "Mary Adoring the Child" or "Holy Night"; or Murillo, "Madonna and Child"; or Raphael, "Sistine Madonna" or "Madonna of the Chair."

It is well to start early planning for a giving project. Allow the group to choose among several ideas presented. Helping a needy family will bring added meaning to Christmas. The boys and girls are able to help with shopping and preparing baskets if the work is done before the rush is on. There is a fine opportunity for personal enrichment within the members of the group if counselors or leaders will supervise the project.

PRELUDE: "Adoration" by Borowski

CALL TO WORSHIP:

> Star of the East, that long ago
> Brought wise men on their way
> Where, angels singing to and fro,
> The Child of Bethlehem lay—

194

WISE MEN BRING THEIR GIFTS

Above that Syrian hill afar
Thou shinest out tonight, O Star!

. . . .

Star of the East! show us the way
   In wisdom undefiled
To seek that manger out and lay
   Our gifts before the child—
To bring our hearts and offer them
Unto Our King in Bethlehem!
          —Eugene Field

Hymn: "The First Noel" or
      "There's a Song in the Air"

Scripture:

Unto us a child is born, unto us a son is given: and the government shall be upon his shoulder: and his name shall be called Wonderful, Counsellor, The mighty God, The everlasting Father, The Prince of Peace.

Now when Jesus was born in Bethlehem of Judaea in the days of Herod the king, behold, there came wise men from the east to Jerusalem, saying, Where is he that is born King of the Jews? for we have seen his star in the east, and are come to worship him. . . . Then Herod, when he had privily called the wise men, enquired of them diligently what time the star appeared. And he sent them to Bethlehem, and said, Go and search diligently for the young child; and when ye have found him, bring me word again, that I may come and worship him also. When they had heard the king, they departed; and, lo, the star, which they saw in the east, went before them, till it came and stood over where the young child was. When they saw the star, they rejoiced with exceeding great joy.

And when they were come into the house, they saw the young child with Mary his mother, and fell down, and worshipped him: and when they had opened their treasures, they presented unto him gifts; gold, and frankincense, and myrrh.[1]

Candlelighting:

As we light this candle, may we do it reverently and with gratitude for the gift of God's Son to the world. As the wise men brought their gifts to the Christ child, may we give in a spirit of love, thinking of

195

the joy we may bring to others instead of what we may receive ourselves.

LEADER:

We will hear the story "The Star Still Shines."

STORY:

THE STAR STILL SHINES

All was silent around the campfire as a group of men looked beyond the light of the fire into the starry heavens. They had allowed the fire to die down to enable them to better see the heavenly glory.

These men were seekers for Truth, and believed it would be revealed to them by some unusual manifestation in the skies. It was a wonderful night, and under the hush that seemed to pervade the earth and the sky they felt that some new revelation was about to be made, and they were eager to receive it.

Suddenly the silence was broken as Casper, one of the group, excitedly cried, "There is a new glory in the heavens tonight. Over yonder shines a new star, more brilliant and more beautiful than any I have ever seen. Behold! it is growing more brilliant each moment, and already outshines every other star. This must be the night of a royal birth, and the new Star is sent to herald the great event. It may even be that it proclaims the birth of the One who will be to all nations, the Way, the Truth, and the Life.

See! it appears to be moving, as if it were beckoning us to leave the fading light of our self-kindled fires and follow to an Everlasting Light which we have long sought, but never found. The fires we have kindled are dying, but the wonderful Star shines brighter and brighter. Let us leave our dying fires, with their fading light, and follow the Star wherever it may guide us. My heart tells me that we shall find the One for whom the world has long waited. Are you ready to come with me, wherever the Star shall lead?"

His companions gave assurance of their willingness, and sought the blessing of God upon their undertaking. Then, under the spell of the beautiful Star, they went to their dwellings to prepare for their great adventure. *And the Star was shining.*

It was necessary to spend a number of days in preparation for the journey. The Wise Men did not know just what experiences they would pass through, or how long would be the journey. They searched their sacred books, and the books of other peoples to discover any prophecy, or message, concerning the Star.

Among the books of the Hebrew people they found an unfulfilled prophecy which said, "And thou, Bethlehem, in the land of Judah, art by no means least among the rulers of Judah; for from thee shall come a ruler who will govern my people Israel."

The Wise Men recalled that the Star had seemed to be beckoning toward the direction in which the little town of Bethlehem was located, but they found it hard to believe that the little town could be the birthplace of a King. Yet the prophet had definitely stated "Bethlehem in the land of Judah."

If the Star should lead them to a new born king they could not appear in his presence empty handed, so they spent much time in getting together gifts which would be worthy of a king, and among the precious gifts were gold, frankincense, and myrrh.

When the evening for their departure came they waited with great anxiety in the darkening eventide for the appearance of the Star. Then, as it appeared in the heavens, they joined in their evening devotions, mounted their camels, and began their journey. *And the Star went before them.*

After some nights of travel under the guidance of the Star, they came near to the great city of Jerusalem. The gold-covered roof of the palace of Herod the king reflected the last rays of the setting sun, as Casper said to his companions, "Our journey is almost over. Here is where we shall find the new-born king. Let us hasten to the palace and offer our gifts." "Behold the Star!" exclaimed Melchior. "It beckons us onward. It does not rest over the city. See! it is moving toward the South. Let us not go to the palace, but follow the Star wherever it may lead."

"But where else would a king be born, except in a palace?" retorted Casper. "True the ancient prophet said that Bethlehem would be honored, but there is no palace in Bethlehem; only flocks of sheep and some poor shepherds. That is no place for a king to be born. Let us move quickly to the palace and inquire."

"If we go into the city, I fear we shall lose the Star," said Melchior. "It is still beckoning us away from Jerusalem. It would be a sorry fate for us to have traveled thus far, and now fail to see the new-born king."

With great emphasis Casper impatiently replied, "Hear me again! Kings are born in palaces. Here is where we shall find the king. Let us hasten to the palace." Casper prevailed over his companions, and they went on to the palace. *And the Star still beckoned.*

Arriving at the palace, the Wise Men inquired, "Where is He who is born King of the Jews? For we have seen his star in the East and have come to worship Him."

The palace guards reported to King Herod the coming of the Wise Men, and how they were seeking a new king of the Jews. Herod ordered them to be brought into his presence, and to him they told the story of the beautiful Star which they had first seen in their homeland, and how it had led them to the land of Judah. They said they had made the long journey to pay homage to the new born king, and desired to know where they might find him.

Herod was greatly disturbed by the story of the Wise Men. He saw his throne in danger, and his cruel reign coming to an end. He questioned the Wise Men carefully to find out just when the Star first appeared. Then he sent for the chief priests and scribes of the people and inquired where the Christ was to be born. They told him that according to the ancient prophets the birth would take place in the little town of Bethlehem. Learning this, Herod spoke privately to the Wise Men and told them to continue their journey by going to Bethlehem. He said, "Go, and search diligently for the child, and when you have found him, bring me word, that I too may come and worship him."

With fear and doubt the Wise Men left the palace of Herod. They were afraid. They were not afraid of Herod the king—cruel tyrant that he was. *They were afraid they might have lost the Star.* They remembered how it had beckoned them onward when they were so sure that a palace was the only place where a king could be born. Maybe the Eternal One would now refuse to give them further light because of their disobedience. They were afraid they might never see the king. So, it was with troubled hearts and minds that they left the palace and made their way through the streets of Jerusalem to the place where their camels were sheltered.

When they were some distance outside the city gate Balthazzar, the third Wise Man, shouted in a voice vibrant with joy, "Behold, my comrades, the Star still shines! The Eternal One is good to us. His goodness is greater than our folly."

"And lo, the star which they had seen in the East went before them, till it came to rest over the place where the child was. When they saw the star they rejoiced exceedingly with great joy; and going into the house they saw the child with Mary his mother, and they fell

198

down and worshipped him. Then opening their treasures they offered him gifts—gold, and frankincense, and myrrh."

The Star had led them to the King.

The hearts of the Wise Men were filled with a deep joy as they began their homeward journey. They did not return by way of Jerusalem because God had revealed to them that King Herod had sent out his soldiers on the terrible mission of slaying all children two years and under. In this way he hoped to destroy the new born king.

When the Wise Men were crossing the plains of Bethlehem they spoke with shepherds who were greatly excited because of events which had recently taken place. They, too, had been to Bethlehem. One of them told the story while the Wise Men listened with amazement. He said, "We were watching our sheep at night, when suddenly the sky became ablaze with glory, and an angel appeared telling us not to be afraid. He said,

" 'I bring you good news of a great joy which shall come to all the people; for to you is born this day in the city of David a Saviour, who is Christ the Lord.'

"He told us we would find the child in a manger. This was hard to believe and as we marvelled there appeared with the angel a multitude of angels singing, 'Glory to God in the highest, and on earth peace among men with whom he is pleased!' When the angels went away we said to one another, 'Let us go over to Bethlehem and see this thing that has happened, which the Lord has made known to us.' We hurried to Bethlehem and found Mary and Joseph in a stable, and they showed us the babe lying in a manger. Now we are praising and glorifying God for all we have seen and heard."

It was still difficult for the Wise Men to believe that the Son of God could be born in a stable, and that the first to adore Him were the humble shepherds of the plains. It was hard to believe the Eternal One would lay aside his majesty and glory to become a babe in a manger.

The first night out from Jerusalem the Wise Men kindled their evening fire and sat in its light, but looking into the heavens which had new meaning for them. Casper was deeply moved as he said, "The heavens will never seem the same again. We have seen the Star and wherever we go we shall forever be in its light. We have seen the King to whom, with our gifts, we gave the devotion of our hearts.

"But how near we came to disaster because we left the light of the Star. Thanks to the Eternal One for revealing to us that a God can be found in a stable. That redeemers are found in other places than palaces. That a manger can be mightier than an empire throne. My comrades, we came near losing everything. In following our own willful way we endangered the child of Bethlehem. Only by the gracious love of God did we find our way. So long as we followed the Star we were secure. When we turned from its light and went our own way we were in danger."

Before dawn the next morning the Wise Men from the East continued homeward. *And the Star was still shining.*[2]

POEM:

If I were a man of ages past,
  A searcher of the signs, increased,
  I'd be a Wise Man from the East,
Before the Christ my treasures cast.

If I were a star above the earth,
  A gem in heaven's diadem,
  I'd be the star of Bethlehem
And light the scene of Jesus' birth.

If I were an Angel, now or then,
  One sent from God his words to bring,
  I'd join the Heavenly Host and sing
Of "peace on earth, good will to men."[3]

—MACK B. STOKES

OFFERTORY:

In our offering we have an opportunity to share with the poor. In your giving you may bring joy to some child who otherwise would have very little at this Christmas season.

As they offered gifts most rare
At that manger rude and bare,
So may we with holy joy,
Pure, and free from sin's alloy,
All our costliest treasures bring,
Christ, to thee, our heavenly King.

—WILLIAM C. DIX

OFFERING

PRAYER:

Our Father, who sent light into the world through the gift of thy Son, may the spirit of Christ come into our lives; make us mindful of the poor, the lonely, the blind, the crippled. Touch our hearts and make us willing to share with the needy the good things that we enjoy. Help us to join that great company of believers who through following Christ have gained strength to serve thee and to live peaceably with all people. Grant that at this Christmas season joy and peace may enter the hearts of many people of the world. Accept our gifts and may we not forget to give ourselves to thee. In Jesus' name we pray. AMEN.

HYMN: "Angels, from the Realms of Glory" or
"Hark! the Herald Angels Sing"

BENEDICTION:

As we go from this service, may thy spirit abide with us and thy love remain in our hearts. AMEN.

SERVICE 33

CHRISTMAS FOR EVERYONE
(*Christmas*)

PRELUDE: Hymn tune "The First Noel"

CALL TO WORSHIP:

> Hark! the glad sound! the Saviour comes,
> The Saviour promised long:
> Let every heart prepare a throne,
> And every voice a song.
>
> .   .   .   .
>
> He comes, the broken heart to bind,
> The bleeding soul to cure,
> And with the treasures of his grace
> To enrich the humble poor.
>
> —PHILIP DODDRIDGE

HYMN: "O Come, All Ye Faithful" or
"It Came upon the Midnight Clear"

PRAYER:

O thou who didst cause light to shine out of darkness in the coming of thy Son to the world, help us to make our hearts ready for thee. Forgive us, if in the celebration of his birth, our thoughts are centered on material things. Forbid that we should crowd thee out of our lives during the rush of this Christmas holiday. Come and rule in our hearts and abide with us forever. In Jesus' name we pray. AMEN.

CHRISTMAS FOR EVERYONE

Scripture:

In the beginning was the Word, . . . and the Word was made flesh, and dwelt among us, (and we beheld his glory. . . .)

When the fulness of the time was come, God sent forth his Son. . . .

For God so loved the world, that he gave his only begotten Son, that whosoever believeth in him should not perish, but have everlasting life.

For God sent not his Son into the world to condemn the world; but that the world through him might be saved.[1]

Story:

THE BLIND SHEPHERD OF BETHLEHEM

My name is Bartimeus, which means "Son of Timeus." I am commonly called "Blind Bartimeus" because I was born blind. . . . I am the son of a shepherd. My father was one of a group of men who cared for sheep on the plains of Bethlehem. When I was but a small boy my father would take me by the hand and allow me to go with him as he led his sheep to green pastures and still waters. As I grew older I got to know many of the well-known sheep paths, although I could not see them. They had become very familiar to me because, with my father, I had walked them so often, and by reason of my blindness I had no other interests like other boys would have.

The Bethlehem shepherds were very kind to me and watched over me in times of danger. There is no heart more kind and more gentle than the heart of a good shepherd.

As a blind boy among the shepherds I had many interesting and unusual experiences; but the greatest of all happened one wonderful night when we were camped near the royal town of Bethlehem.

It was a thrilling experience for me because, for the first time, my father had given me permission to remain all night with the shepherds. . . . How I enjoyed helping with the sheep at the close of the day. My father allowed me to stand at the door of the fold where I could feel the sheep as one by one they came along. I took briars from their wool and thorns from their feet, and then reached to the water and gave each one an overflowing cup. I never thought of my blindness while I was trying to be a shepherd.

After the evening tasks were finished we joined in evening worship, for the shepherd is a devout man. As the lengthening shadows fell over the Bethlehem plains I listened to my father as he very reverently repeated the words of our great King David, who also was a shepherd.

"The Lord is my shepherd; I shall not want.
He maketh me to lie down in green pastures:
He leadeth me beside the still waters.
He restoreth my soul:
He leadeth me in the paths of righteousness
    for his name's sake.
Yea, though I walk through the valley of the
    shadow of death,
I will fear no evil: for thou art with me;
Thy rod and thy staff they comfort me.
Thou preparest a table before me in the
    presence of mine enemies:
Thou anointest my head with oil;
My cup runneth over.
Surely goodness and mercy shall follow me
    all the days of my life:
And I will dwell in the house of the Lord for ever."
"O magnify the Lord with me, and let us exalt his
    name together.
O taste and see that the Lord is good; blessed is
    the man that trusteth in him."

Reverently each shepherd waited in silence before the Eternal One, as a holy hush seemed to fall over the evening. When men are listening to God, lips are silent.

Later, one of the shepherds, Ben-Joseph by name, broke the silence as he said, "God's people have waited long. When will the Messiah appear? The cruel Roman holds us in bondage and the chosen of God are governed by one who fears not Jehovah. . . . Has God forgotten his people?"

To which another shepherd, Ben-Aaron, replied, "Strange that you should ask, Ben-Joseph, what was in my heart to speak. Truly Messiah tarries, but let us not sin against God through lack of faith. The promise of Jehovah is sure and will not be broken. The coming Messiah may not be far off. We know not the mind of the Eternal One. He may delay his coming, but in the fulness of time Messiah will redeem his people. The Day of the Lord may be nearer than we think."

Even as he spoke something happened. I heard some of the shepherds cry out in fear, and from the sound of their movements I sensed that they had thrown themselves to the ground. I cried out to know what had happened, but no word came from the shepherds. Then I

called louder, "Father, tell me what has happened. Reach out your
hand and touch me for I am sore afraid." Then I heard a voice, sweet
and beautiful which said, "Be not afraid; for behold I bring you good
news of a great joy which will come to all people; for to you is born
this day in the city of David, a Savior, who is Christ the Lord. And
this shall be a sign for you; you will find a babe wrapped in
swaddling clothes and lying in a manger." And suddenly there was
with the angel a multitude of the heavenly host praising God and
saying, "Glory to God in the highest, and on earth peace among men
with whom he is pleased!" *Angel*

I heard the shepherds echo the words as one by one they said,
"Glory to God! Glory to God!" Then my father said, "Let us go
over to Bethlehem and see this thing that has happened, which the
Lord has made known unto us. One of us must remain with the
sheep, and with him we will leave Bartimeus. The rest of us will go
over to Bethlehem."

At this I cried out, "My father, do not leave me. I would know
what has come to pass, even though I am unable to see. Do not leave
me because of my blindness. I, too, would go to Bethlehem!" My
father's hand gripped mine and I could feel it tremble as we started
across the plain to the City of David.

When we got to the town I listened as the shepherds persuaded
the watchman to allow us to enter. They told him of the words of
the angel that a Savior had been born in Bethlehem. They told him
of the lighted heavens and the chorus of music, but he would not
believe them. He had heard nothing except the noise of the revelers
who were there for the enrollment. He told them there was a light
in the stable of the Bethlehem Inn and suggested they go there to
enquire about the birth of a child, and added, "But that is no place
to find a Messiah."

Stumbling through the dark streets we came to a place which I
knew was the stable because of the smell of cattle and camels. My
father kept hold of my hand and guided me step by step as we entered. Then he pressed his other hand on my shoulder and said,
"Kneel, my son, and adore him, Christ the Lord!"

In my blindness I sank to my knees. I could see nothing, but
my young heart told me that I was in the Divine presence. I trembled as I said to myself, "The Messiah is here and I am unable to see
him. I am blind!"

We returned to the plains and kept watch over the sheep for the
rest of the night. I listened eagerly to every description the shep-

herds gave of the wonderful evening, and I tried to understand what they had seen. How I wished I could see! It's a terrible thing to be blind!

A few days after when I had been left alone on the plain, I heard the sound of approaching camel bells. It would have been good to see the camels which had no doubt come from some faraway land. I was greatly surprised when they came nearer and one of the men said, "Boy of Bethlehem, where is he who is born King of the Jews? For we have seen his star in the East and have come to worship Him. We bring gifts of gold, frankincense, and myrrh."

I told him of the singing angels and the wonderful music, and also about the things the shepherds had seen. Then I told him of our visit to Bethlehem where we had found the child in the manger. When I spoke about the manger, one of the men impatiently said, "Heed not the talk of a blind shepherd boy, let us hasten to Jerusalem and there in the royal palace we shall no doubt find the new born king." So they left me, and as the tinkling of the camel bells grew fainter, how I wished I could have seen them. But, . . . I was blind!

The years that followed were cruel years for me. My father and mother died and I was left alone—truly alone—in my blindness. Without my father's hand to lead me I was of little use to the shepherds, and they no longer allowed me to journey with them to the pasture lands. I was useless and unwanted. Just blind Bartimeus.

There was only one way I knew to keep my growing body alive. I must become a beggar, sit by the side of the Jericho Road and in my blindness call on those who were passing to give me alms. So, year after year as a growing boy and through early manhood, I sat by the side of the road—a blind beggar. Few people stopped to greet me and tell me of things which were taking place. . . .

One day a man gave me a coin, and, to my joy stopped to talk with me. He was excited about a journey he had recently taken to the north country of Galilee, where he had seen and heard a wonder-working teacher called Jesus of Nazareth. He told of the wonderful works wrought by Jesus, and how he had even made the blind to see. As he told about the wonderful things I said, "O that he would pass this way!"

Then came the day of days! It began like all others. Early in the morning I found my way to the Jericho Road hoping it would be a good day. I measured the days by the number and value of the coins given to me by those who went by. Because of the increasing numbers of the Passover crowds I was sure the day would be a good one.

Toward noon there was a lot of unusual travel on the Jericho Road, and the crowd became so great that I felt men pushing and crowding where I sat. When I enquired about the reason for the unusual excitement in the crowd I was told "Jesus of Nazareth is passing by!" For a moment I did not recognize the name, or associate it with the wonder-working prophet, but when I did I cried out with a loud voice, "Jesus, Son of David, have pity on me!" Those in front of me rebuked me, telling me to be silent; but I cried out all the more, "Son of David, have mercy on me!" Then I heard music more beautiful than the singing of the angels at Bethlehem. It was the voice of Jesus of Nazareth as he said, "Bring him to me." The people turned to me and said: "Take heart. Rise! He is calling you."

I threw off my beggar's mantle and stood in his presence, blind and trembling. Then Jesus said, "What do you want me to do for you?" and I said to him, "Master, let me receive my sight." And Jesus said to me, "Go your way, your faith has made you well," and immediately I could see! I am no longer blind Bartimeus! . . . I have seen the Christ! [2]

POEM:

    O holy star of Bethlehem
    That guided wise-men all the way,
    Lead us along the path with them
    To find the Prince of Peace, we pray.

    O heavenly host whose "Gloria"
    Gave hope to lowly shepherds then,
    Sing us again your "Gloria"
    And "Peace on earth, good will toward men."

    O Lord of all Whose life divine
    Brought heaven to earth in days of old,
    Exalt once more this love of Thine
    That all the world Thyself behold.[3]
                       —MACK B. STOKES

PRAYER:

Our Father, whose love to us is shown in the gift of thy Son, guide us as we try to bring joy to some of thy children. Help us to be messengers of good will by being friendly to the lonely, kind to the unfortunate, and sharing with the needy. Come into our lives and show us how to use our talents and means to carry the good news of the gospel to those who are still in darkness. May the joy of the Christmas season enter every home and help us to grow in the knowledge of Christ in the days that are ahead. In the name of the Prince of Peace we pray. AMEN.

HYMN: "O Little Town of Bethlehem" or
        "Silent Night, Holy Night"

BENEDICTION:

Dismiss us with thy blessing and prepare our hearts to receive the Christ child. AMEN.

SERVICE 34

WHEN TRIALS COME
(*Communion Sunday*)

Each person finds his own path to God, but there is a fellowship we feel with our fellow men as we consecrate ourselves in God's service in the act of Communion. We should come to God in humility, ask his blessings on all who work together to bring his kingdom on earth.

In the worship center use a cross with lighted candles. If the poems in this service are memorized and read with proper expression, the service will be more effective. If the poems must be read, the reader should be in the back of the room or out of sight, so the handling of papers will not be a distraction. Special music will add to the effectiveness of the service. If given at camp or out of doors, the cross may be made of a limb with the bark left on, or of roughhewn lumber.

PRELUDE: Hymn tune "Londonderry"

CALL TO WORSHIP:
> Thou camest, O Lord, with the living word
>   That should set thy people free;
> But with mocking scorn, and with crown of thorn,
>   They bore thee to Calvary.
> —EMILY E. S. ELLIOTT

HYMN: "Beneath the Cross of Jesus" or
  " 'Tis Midnight; and on Olive's Brow"

SCRIPTURE:
He is despised and rejected of men; a man of sorrows, and acquainted with grief. . . . All we like sheep have gone astray; we have turned every one to his own way; and the Lord hath laid on him the

iniquity of us all. . . . He is brought as a lamb to the slaughter, and as a sheep before her shearers is dumb, so he openeth not his mouth. . . .

And Pilate, when he had called together the chief priests and the rulers of the people, said unto them, Ye have brought this man unto me, as one that perverteth the people: and, behold, I, having examined him before you, have found no fault in this man touching those things whereof ye accuse him. . . .

Pilate therefore, willing to release Jesus, spake again to them. But they cried, saying, Crucify him, crucify him. . . . As they led him away, they laid hold upon one Simon, a Cyrenian, coming out of the country, and on him they laid the cross, that he might bear it after Jesus.[1]

HYMN: "Into the Woods My Master Went" (May be sung as a solo)

POEM:

I WAS THERE

Yes, I carried his cross to Golgotha.
They made me carry it. I refused it as long as I dared.
But black men cannot always refuse the white man's orders.
Little people cannot resist the powerful people forever.
We are finally forced to submit, to obey.
Some force us with whips. We yield and hate.
Some force us with kindness. We yield and love.
That happened to me that day in Jerusalem.

I had just arrived from Cyrene.
I was walking along the street when I heard a frightening, rumbling sound.
It sounded like thunder. But the sky was clear.
Then I recognized human voices, angry voices, sobbing voices.
Then I saw the procession.
At the head of this slow-moving company was a tall, slender man.
He was dragging a cross too heavy for his frail body.
He stumbled and fell. And he didn't get up.
A Roman soldier struck him with his whip, but he couldn't get up.

WHEN TRIALS COME

He was down to stay.
He lifted his head and looked around as if hoping some
    friend would help him.
Some women wiped the blood from his face.
They tried to lift the cross. But it was too heavy
    for them.

I wanted to run away. And yet something held me there.
I couldn't take my eyes from his face.
I wished I had never come to Jerusalem.
And yet, I was glad that I was there.
Then the Roman centurion saw me.
I knew instantly what he intended to do.
He came striding toward me, his face hard and cruel.
I could not move!
The hatred of my heart drove hot blood to my head.
I wanted to drive my two big fists into that evil,
    sneering face.
How I hated him and all he stood for in that moment!
And yet I felt pity for him.
Maybe he hated this job.
Maybe he did not relish his work.
All he knew was to obey orders.
I looked past the centurion and saw that man pinned
    to the stones of the street by the heavy cross.
The centurion shouted his order at me angrily: "You,
    black man! Come and carry this cross to Golgotha!"

"No!" I shouted. "No! I will not. I am not of Jerusalem.
    I am not your black man."
But even as I spoke I knew that I would carry that cross
    to Golgotha.
I would carry it—not because the centurion ordered me,
    nor because the soldiers could punish me with their
    whips and swords.
I would bear that cross because some strange power drew
    me to the man who looked so helpless and alone.
He needed someone to lift that load from his back.
But more . . . he needed a friend!
And I felt I wanted to be his friend!

I stepped into the street and toward him.

The centurion followed me.

I forgot all who were watching.

It was as if just the man under the cross and I were
there alone . . . just the two of us.

As I stopped to shift the cross from his back to my
shoulders he smiled.

He spoke quietly to me, "Thanks! My brother!"

A strange strength surged through my body. I felt I
could have carried the gates and walls of Jerusalem
in that moment.

I was no longer just a black man. I felt I was a son of God!

"Thanks! My brother!"

For the first time in my life I was not conscious that
I was black!

I do not remember the walk up Golgotha's hill.

I cannot recall carrying the cross.

Other arms and shoulders must have borne its weight.

There were just two of us walking that sad way that day . . .
just he and I.

I followed him . . . and felt that what I was doing was
right and good.

On the hill, I felt shame for the priests in their
ceremonial robes.

I was sorry for the people who jeered, "Let his blood
be upon us . . . !"

They did not know what they were saying.

The only person on the hill who needed no pity was
this tall, slender man.

But—a great change came over him as he stood there waiting.

He no longer looked frail and lonely.

He appeared refreshed, sure of himself, unprotesting, unafraid.

I was proud of him!

Then . . . he did something so unexpected that everyone
gasped.

The priests looked at each other with misgivings and fear.

The soldiers were stunned and stood uneasy waiting their
orders.

That man with the crown of thorns on his head, and

bloodstains on his face, walked deliberately to the cross
where I had dropped it.
He looked down on it for a moment.
Then . . . he turned and lay down on it as if lying down
for a nap.
No one could breathe for a moment.
The centurion stared in amazement.
Finally, in a harsh whisper, he ordered the guards to
to do their work.
Hurriedly they pounded the nails into his hands and feet.

I had seen many punishments, brutal and evil.
But I had never seen a crucifixion.
My teeth bit into my lips until I tasted blood.
Those nails went right through his hands . . . into my
heart.
I closed my eyes to shut out the cruel scene.
I fell to my knees.
I prayed that God would forgive all these people who
did not realize what they were doing.
He did not struggle.
No word of protest, no cry of pain came from his lips.
As I knelt, weeping—and hating the men who had done
this thing to him—the soldiers dropped his cross
into its socket . . . between two thieves.

I came close to him then.
I wanted him to know that I was his friend to the very end.
His lips moved. I could not hear all that he said.
He seemed to be talking to someone very near.
He looked at me and smiled, as if saying again,
"Thanks! My brother!"
Once more I felt that strange power surge through me.
I felt like a new man!
All the evil deeds I had ever done were now forgiven
and forgotten.
All the hatred and resentment I had ever felt were
gone out of me.
I was born again! I was free!
I loved everybody!

Nobody could ever again hurt me!
I never dreamed that my name would be known beyond
  Cyrene.
What I did that day in Jerusalem, I did for him . . .
  and for him alone! [2]

—CHESTER A. McPHEETERS

POEM:

Here, O Christ, our sins we see,
  Learn thy love while gazing thus;
Sin, which laid the cross on thee,
  Love, which bore the cross for us.

Here we learn to serve and give,
  And, rejoicing, self deny;
Here we gather love to live,
  Here we gather faith to die.

Pressing onward as we can,
  Still to this our hearts must tend;
Where our earliest hopes began,
  There our last aspirings end;

Till amid the hosts of light,
  We in thee redeemed, complete,
Through thy cross made pure and white,
  Cast our crowns before thy feet.

—ELIZABETH R. CHARLES

PRAYER:

Our Father, as we think of Christ accepting the Cross willingly, help us to be ready to sacrifice for the things we believe are right. Forbid that we should neglect to call upon thee when things go well with us, but may we with open minds come to thee daily for guidance and for courage to do what seems right. We are sorry for our mistakes and blunders. Grant us strength and determination to uproot our faults and weaknesses and live by the highest and best we know. May we not drift along in our own wisdom and fail to seek help from thee. Help us to know what is right and to follow the example of Christ in our daily living. In his name we pray. AMEN.

WHEN TRIALS COME

COMMUNION SERVICE (conducted by the minister)

HYMN: "In the Cross of Christ I Glory" or
"When I Survey the Wondrous Cross"

BENEDICTION:
May the spirit of Christ remain with us, guiding and directing us as we go from this service. AMEN.

SERVICE 35

SON OF STEPHEN [1]
(*A Play*)
By Clyde Cruse

The following play may be a complete worship service and should be presented in a reverent mood. It may be given as effectively in a one-room church as in a more elaborate auditorium. If the sanctuary is used, the pulpit furniture may be taken out or hidden by screens. Lighting effects should receive special attention. The furniture used should be simple, such as might have been in a boy's room in the first century.

Intermediate boys and girls may take all of the parts, but the girl taking the part of Sarah should dress and be made up to appear older. Loose flowing costumes in bright colors, together with sandals such as were used in the time of Christ, should be worn.

Those taking part should set aside sufficient time to learn their parts and to act in harmony with the characters they portray. Do not over-act, but try to feel the thoughts and emotions expressed in the lines. Sincerity on the part of the boys and girls will add much to the effectiveness of the play.

The worship service should begin with an appropriate congregational or choral hymn, followed by a brief and suitably worded prayer. If no printed leaflets are supplied, a simple statement could give the setting, time, place, and characters of the play. A Scripture selection, Acts 7:54-60, should then precede another choral or instrumental offering to set the mood of reverent attention.

SON OF STEPHEN

SETTING:

A few hours earlier, a mob aroused to fury toward Stephen because of his pointed preaching concerning Jesus, has stoned him to death outside the gates of Jerusalem. Among those present, and giving consent to their action, was Saul of Tarsus, who later became the apostle, Paul.

CHARACTERS:

Sarah, the wife of Stephen, a devout woman
David, their son, a stalwart youth of about 18
Elizabeth and Esther, their daughters, also in their teens
Jotham and Nathan, friends of David

PLACE:

David's room in the home of Stephen. It contains a couch, stools, a table and a chest for clothing. An entrance at *left* leads to the rest of the house; one at *right* leads outside.

TIME:

About dusk on a day in the year A.D. 33.

(As the play opens, Sarah is bowed in deep grief, seated on the floor with her head upon the couch. Elizabeth and Esther are trying to comfort her. Sarah's voice is strained and weak. She raises her head and bravely brushes away her tears.)

THE PLAY

SARAH: Why does not David come? At such a time as this, I need my son, and surely he needs me. What if he, too, has fallen into the hands of evil men?

ELIZABETH: Please do not worry, mother. David will come soon. He is almost a man, and knows the city well. No harm will come to him.

ESTHER: Perhaps he lingers to be sure our father's body is receiving proper care and preparation for burial by our friends.

ELIZABETH: Will you not come and see how many are already gathered here to share our grief? Oh, it is good to know the love they bear us in this dreadful time!

SARAH: Good daughter, go and tell them I will come. But I cannot rest till I see David. He loved his father so! I know not what wild dreams may come to him in consequence of seeing his father beaten to death with cruel stones. I wish within my soul that David had not happened to be there.

217

(Elizabeth goes out, *left*. As Sarah rises with Esther's help, Jotham enters, *right*. He hesitates just inside the door.)

SARAH: Jotham! O good friend of David, have you seen my son? He has not come since—Since—Do you know the tragedy that has befallen us?

JOTHAM: Alas, respected mother of my dearest friend, I know. Only two well I know, for I, too, saw it even as did David. It was too frightful to behold and keep my peace. I vowed to have revenge, and so did David.

SARAH: Oh, no! Revenge is not my wish. My husband prayed for those who cast the stones, and so do I. Our faith in Christ has given us the power to forgive, just as our Lord himself forgave and prayed for those who nailed him to the cross. You must go to David—tell him this for me.

(She bows and tensely clasps her hands.)

ESTHER: Jotham, where *is* David now?

JOTHAM: I cannot tell you, Esther, for I have just come to meet him here. He asked me to come at nightfall—Nathan, too. Has Nathan come?

ESTHER: I have not seen him. Mother, we must go. I will bring David to you when he comes.

SARAH: Very well, my daughter. But someone must tell him that another hateful act cannot bring Stephen back to us. Surely he must be beside himself, in so sudden and so great a sorrow. But he must listen! This is a time when God alone can give the help we need.

(Elizabeth enters, *left,* in time to hear Sarah's last statement.)

ELIZABETH: And God *is* helping, mother. He has sent our good friend, John, the disciple of our Lord. He wants to speak with you.

SARAH: Oh, I am glad he came! His counsel now can be my guide—and David's too. Jotham tells me he will be home soon.

ELIZABETH: Oh, that is good! Thank you, Jotham.

(Jotham bows acknowledgment. Sarah goes out, *left,* with Elizabeth and Esther, who turn at the door.)

ESTHER: (To Jatham) Please tell us when my brother comes.

(She goes out. Jotham does not seem to hear. Nervously he walks about. After a moment Nathan enters, *right*.)

NATHAN: (A little breathless) I was delayed. There is much talk and much excitement. All Jerusalem is astir. Where is David?

JOTHAM: He has not come. His mother is worried. Have you not seen him since we separated at the city gate?

NATHAN: No. He hurried away, I know not where. He only told me to come here, as he told you.

JOTHAM: I came at sunset, as he wished. I am prepared—for anything. Are you?

NATHAN: (Grimly) Yes. My life, if need be, is at David's call. He would do as much for me, I know.

JOTHAM: That is true. We three have been as brothers all these years. And now, though not yet men, we have to play the part of warriors. If we die, we shall not die alone!

NATHAN: But how can we take vengeance on a mob? This troubles me. Can we seek out and slay each man who cast a stone at Stephen?

JOTHAM: David will have a plan. I know of one he will not overlook— that surly Saul of Tarsus. He who stood so righteously while others drew the blood of David's father. Did you see him?

NATHAN: Yes. I know him well.

JOTHAM: David pointed out this man and said to me, "He is the fiercest Pharisee of all. 'Tis he who should be in my father's place, for he imprisons those whose only crime is that they love and serve the Christ. Now his hands drip blood, for that he holds the garments of those bloody men." Those were David's words, and more than once he swore that Saul should pay.

NATHAN: I heard him. And I also fear this Saul. I know that he will yet do all he can to kill our faith. Will it be wrong then if we kill him first?

JOTHAM: I say not wrong. I would myself perform the act, but David first must have his chance.

NATHAN: Could he not use his sling? His skill is great enough to hit a coin posted at a dozen paces. I will spy out the habits of this man, to set a time and place to take him by surprise. Possibly at break of day when he sets out to seek more followers of the way our Master taught.

JOTHAM: Good thinking, Nathan. David's idol was his father, Stephen, but his hero is the great King David, who of old was master of the sling. Like the one whose name he bears, our friend has practiced to perfection with such stones as felled Goliath. He could send swift silent death unto this evil persecutor.

NATHAN: No doubt this very thing is in his mind. And by the way, I chanced to see this Saul awhile ago as I came by the Inn. He acted strangely. For while others ate and drank he sat in stony silence, as if pondering the bloody scene outside the city gate. He was apart, and had it been quite dark I could so easily have sent a spear into him.

JOTHAM: Nay, it is too soon! We must wait, and keep our counsel, weighing with great care what we shall do. David's mother is against his taking vengeance. I will warn him to pretend that nothing is afoot. Doubtless he will hold his peace until the time of mourning is complete. Then we will indeed have satisfaction!

NATHAN: (Looking out) I see David coming. But his tread is slow. He does not appear the same as when we left him.

JOTHAM: (Going to the door to see) You are right. But that is no surprise. To undergo an ordeal such as this could shatter anyone. Since David is not yet a man, and is both kind and good, no doubt he is appalled at what he now must do. But he will do it!

(They step back as David enters, *right*. He sees them but sits down and bows his head. Puzzled, Jotham and Nathan look at one another.)

NATHAN: Good friend David, are you ill?

(David shakes his head, but does not look up.)

JOTHAM: We have come, as you desired. But if you wish, we will go. Another time can serve to make our plans.

DAVID: (Looking up) Plans? Yes—I had a plan.

JOTHAM: Good. And we are ready. Will you use your sling? Saul of Tarsus is a target worthy of your skill.

NATHAN: I will find out a time when you can slay the arrogant pursuer of the friends of Jesus. We will stand boldly by your side, or hide you afterward if that is your desire.

DAVID: (As if he had not heard, and smiling faintly) Did you see my father as he died? How his face did shine—like unto angels! In the anguish of beholding that so fearful scene, I did not realize it was for him no pain, no torture as it did appear. It was his hour of glory. This I knew was true when I did think upon it later in the temple, where I fled.

JOTHAM: (Astounded) No pain, you say? As stones did beat upon him, shattering his bones and gashing ugly wounds from which his blood did flow to cover him as though it were a crimson mantle? Was he then insensible to savage blows that ground his life away?

DAVID: (Proudly) He felt it, to be sure. But he was glad to be accounted worthy so to die. I know that now. He has told me often how he loved the Lord who died for us upon the cross, and how he wished to be found worthy of such holy love. He said that he would gladly suffer death himself if necessary for the Master's sake.

NATHAN: Yes, he did say that. I heard him, too.

JOTHAM: (Impatiently) I care not what he said. It is unjust and cruel that so innocent a man as he should die the way of hated evildoers. David, I still say your father's murder must be paid for with the killers' blood. You are no weakling. Come now, let us play the part of men!

DAVID: (Gently) I *was* weak, Jotham. Weak enough to want to take men's lives and send their wicked souls to hell. But in the temple I found strength. There, in a quiet corner while the city raged without, I found peace. With it all, I was exhausted, and I barely could get home. But there is no vengeance in my soul.

(Jotham starts to protest more but wilts into frustration. David rises and puts an arm about him.)

DAVID: Jotham, I know how you feel, and I love you for it. Three short hours ago, I felt the same, and I would have slain them one and all.

JOTHAM: (Pleadingly) Why, then, did you change? What has happened?

DAVID: As I wrestled with my thoughts and plans, suddenly I knew that I was not alone.

NATHAN: Someone found you? Who?

DAVID: I am not sure. Possibly it was my father, but I think it was the Lord. Anyway, I was reminded of some words I had been taught . . . "Avenge not thyself" . . . and "Vengeance is mine, I will repay, saith the Lord."

NATHAN: Did you—see anyone?

DAVID: I saw no one with these mortal eyes, nor did he speak except within my mind. But so clearly I remembered how, in dying, Jesus also prayed the Father to "forgive them, for they know not what they do." Then I knew what Spirit made my father say today, as dying he did pray, "Lord, lay not this sin to their charge." If he forgives them, so can I.

JOTHAM: And Saul of Tarsus—he who direly threatens all believers in the Lord, who breathes out fire against those who walk in Jesus' way—will you not try to stop him? You, whose father felt his fury most severely?

DAVID: (Serenely) No. It is God's business—not mine.

JOTHAM: (With resignation) Then I must go. I'm sorry that I cannot share your change of mind. Farewell.

(He goes out, *right*.)

DAVID: I am sorry, too. Farewell, my friend.

NATHAN: David, I can see it as you do—though I would stand beside you if you did intend to kill.

DAVID: Thank you, Nathan. Jotham will in time accept it, too. He will know the meaning of the Master's words: "Love your enemies. Do good to them that hate you, pray for them that despitefully use you, and persecute you. In so doing you will heap coals of fire upon their heads."

NATHAN: What did he mean by that?

DAVID: I think that those who hate you may be able to withstand your hatred in return, but they cannot long resist your love.

ESTHER: (Offstage, *left*) David! Are you here?

DAVID: Yes, my sister, I am here. Nathan, too.

ESTHER: (Entering, *left*) Greetings, Nathan. And is Jotham gone? (To David) He did not tell me when you came. Mother needs you, David. She is much distressed. (Taking his hand) Are you all right?

DAVID: Oh, yes! All is well. Is that not so, friend Nathan?

NATHAN: (Smiling) It is indeed. (To Esther) Your mother needs to have no fear.

DAVID: Where is she? I will go to her now.

ESTHER: There is a company of mourners here, with the disciple, John. They are about to pray.

NATHAN: Will they ask God to bring your father back alive?

ESTHER: No. His death we all accept without complaint. We are agreed to pray for Saul, and others who were there today—the ones for whom my father prayed.

DAVID: (With a triumphant look) For Saul! Yes . . . I, too, can pray for Saul. It is the way to turn our grief into more glory for the Lord. (He takes Esther's hand as they go out, *left*. Nathan follows, glancing upward with a smile.)

NOTES

SERVICE 1. GOD SPEAKS THROUGH A SCIENTIST
1. Ps. 91:1-2.
2. Ps. 104:1-2, 5, 13-14, 24, 33.
3. Used by permission.
4. Adapted from "His Name Is Linked with Peanuts" by John O. Gross in *The Christian Advocate*, September 4, 1941.
5. From *Five New Hymns for Youth by Youth*, copyright 1955 by the Hymn Society of America, used by permission.

SERVICE 2. GOD SPEAKS THROUGH MUSIC
1. Ps. 95:1-2, 6.
2. Ps. 96:1-9.
3. Used by permission of the Hymn Society of America. The folder *Four More New Hymns for Youth by Youth*, in which this hymn may be found, may be obtained from the Hymn Society of America, 297 Fourth Ave., New York 10, at 5 cents each.
4. Used by permission. From *International Journal of Religious Education*.

SERVICE 3. GOD SPEAKS THROUGH SERVICE
1. Rom. 12:1-2; Matt. 20:26-28; 6:24.
2. Matt. 6:19-21.
3. Send offering to Berry School, Mount Berry, Georgia.

SERVICE 4. GOD SPEAKS THROUGH SELF-CONTROL
1. Eccl. 12:1, 13-14; I Tim. 4:12, 14.
2. Prov. 16:32; Ps. 143:10; Prov. 4:23; Ps. 141:4; Prov. 4:24; Ps. 141:3; Prov. 4:20-22; Ps. 119:33-34.
3. By Elizabeth Shafer. From *This Day* Magazine. Used by permission of the author and of Concordia Publishing House.
4. Matt. 5:38-42; Luke 6:31-32, 35.

SERVICE 5. GOD SPEAKS THROUGH NATURE
1. Used by permission.
2. Pss. 104:24; 8:3-6, 9.
3. Matt. 6:30.
4. "Out of the Vast." William Myers, p. 111.
5. "There's Immeasurably More."
6. Used by permission of the Hymn Society of America. From the folder *Four More New Hymns for Youth by Youth* that may be obtained at 5 cents each from the Hymn Society of America, 297 Fourth Ave., New York, N.Y. This hymn may be sung to the tune "Blairgowrie" ("O Young and Fearless Prophet of Ancient Galilee").
7. Used by permission.

SERVICE 6. GOD SPEAKS THROUGH PATRIOTS
1. John 14:6; 18:38, 37; 8:32; 10:10.

SERVICE 7. GOD SPEAKS THROUGH CRUSADERS
1. Ps. 43:3; John 16:13; Prov. 14:34; Ps. 33:12.
2. From *Developing Christian Personality* by Sterling W. Brown. Used by permission of the author and the Christian Board of Publication.

WORSHIP SERVICES FOR JUNIOR HIGHS

SERVICE 8. GOD SPEAKS THROUGH FRIENDS
1. Ps. 11:4.
2. Matt. 22:35-40; John 13:34-35; I Cor. 13:4-8. From the Revised Standard Version of the Bible, Copyrighted 1946 and 1952.
3. Copyrighted by Guideposts Associates, Inc. Guideposts is an inspirational monthly magazine for all faiths published at Carmel, New York. $2.00 per year.

SERVICE 9. GOD SPEAKS THROUGH PEACEMAKERS
1. Ps. 67:3-4.
2. Mic. 4:2, 3; Ps. 37:37; Matt. 5:9.

SERVICE 10. SEEK AND YOU WILL FIND
1. Gen. 28:16, 17; Ps. 95:6.
2. Ps. 84:1-4, 10; Isa. 40:31.
3. Mal. 3:10.
4. From *Adult Student,* April, 1954, p. 15. Methodist Church School Publications. Used by permission.
5. From *The Pilgrim Hymnal.* Copyright, The Pilgrim Press. Used by permission.

SERVICE 11. WE WOULD SEE JESUS
1. From *New Worship and Song.* Copyright, The Pilgrim Press. Used by permission.
2. Luke 2:40, 51; Deut. 6:4-5; 5:7-21; Ps. 19:1-4. From the Revised Standard Version of the Bible, Copyrighted 1946 and 1952.
3. "They Knew Him." From Methodist Church School Publications, copyright Pierce and Washabaugh. Used by permission.
4. From *New Worship and Song.* Copyright, The Pilgrim Press. Used by permission.
5. *Ibid.*
6. From *Guideposts,* January, 1958, p. 4.
7. Used by permission.

SERVICE 12. THE POTENTIAL IN EACH OF US
1. John 15:1-14.
2. Luke 19:1-9.
3. From the *International Journal of Religious Education,* May, 1957, p. 34. Used by permission.

SERVICE 13. FRIENDS OF ALL
1. From "For the Beauty of the Earth."
2. John 15:12-15; Prov. 17:17.
3. Adapted from John 4:9-26, 29.
4. Used by permission.

SERVICE 14. FELLOW WORKMEN WITH GOD
1. "Earth's Common Things."
2. I Tim. 6:12; Ps. 27:14; Deut. 31:6.
3. Used by permission of the Hymn Society of America. From the folder *Four More New Hymns for Youth by Youth* that may be obtained at 5 cents each from the Hymn Society of America, 297 Fourth Ave., New York, N.Y. This hymn may be sung to the tune "Quebec" (O Love Divine, That Stooped to Share.")
4. "What I Live For."

SERVICE 15. HOW SHALL WE CHOOSE OUR WORK?
1. Matt. 20:25-28; 6:24.

SERVICE 16. FAITH GIVES COURAGE
1. From *In Memoriam.*
2. Heb. 11:1-6, 8-10, 13, 16.

NOTES

3. From "The Castle Builder."
4. From "A Child's Offering" in *The Book of Praise for Children.*
5. *Ultima Veritas.* Used by permission of the Columbus School for Girls.
6. Used by permission of the Hymn Society of America. From the folder *Four More New Hymns for Youth by Youth* that may be obtained at 5 cents each from the Hymn Society of America, 297 Fourth Ave., New York, N.Y. This hymn may be sung to the tune "Sandon" ("Lead, Kindly Light").

SERVICE 17. BUILDING IN GOD'S PLAN

1. Ps. 119:15-16.
2. Copyright, 1936, by Purd E. Deitz. Used by permission.
3. I Cor. 3:9-17. From the Revised Standard Version of the Bible, Copyrighted 1946 and 1952.
4. Used by permission.

SERVICE 18. GROWING IN GOD'S PLAN

1. Ps. 95:6-7.
2. Ps. 1.
3. By Graham Hodges. From *50 Children's Sermons.* Used by permission of Abingdon Press.
4. "Look Well to the Growing Edge" from *The Growing Edge.* Used by permission of the author and Harper & Bros.

SERVICE 19. LIVING WITH YOURSELF

1. Phil. 3:12-14; 4:8. From the Revised Standard Version of the Bible, Copyrighted 1946 and 1952.
2. From *Hamlet.*
3. From *Sir Galahad.*
4. From "Alumnus Football."
5. By Anna D. White. From *The Friendly Story Caravan.* Collected by A Committee of the Philadelphia Yearly Meeting of Friends, Anna Pettit Broomell, Chairman. Copyright, 1935, 1948, 1949 by Anna Pettit Broomell. Published by J. B. Lippincott Company. Used by permission.

SERVICE 20. OPENING CLOSED DOORS

1. I John 4:7.
2. Matt. 5:13-16, 43-44, 48.
3. From *International Journal of Religious Education,* January, 1955.
4. II Cor. 9:7.
5. Send offering to Piney Woods Country Life School, Piney Woods, Mississippi.

SERVICE 21. AN URGENT REQUEST

1. Ps. 119:11, 15-16, 33-34, 105; II Tim. 3:14-17.
2. Adapted from *Endless Line of Splendor* by Halford E. Luccock.
3. Matt. 5:3-12.
4. Send offering to American Bible Society, 450 Park Ave., New York 22, N.Y.

SERVICE 22. SHARING THE GOOD NEWS

1. Acts 13:47; Mal. 1:11.
2. Matt. 9:37-38; John 10:16; Luke 13:29; Matt. 28:18-20; Acts 10:34-35.

SERVICE 23. ONE LIFE TO GIVE

1. Matt. 23:9, 8; Acts. 17:26; Matt. 7:12; Ps. 95:6.
2. Isa. 61:1-3; John 3:14, 15, 16.
3. Adapted from "Toyohiko Kagawa: Enchanted by Love," by Roger Ortmayer, from *Christian Action,* January-March, 1957.

WORSHIP SERVICES FOR JUNIOR HIGHS

SERVICE 24. A GIFT FROM MOTHERS
1. Prov. 31:10-11, 26-28.
2. I John 4:7, 11; Exod. 20:12; Col. 3:20.
3. By Laurence C. Jones. Copyright 1956 by The Reader's Digest Association, Inc. Reprinted with permission.
4. Used by permission.
5. Adapted from "A Victorious Life" and used by permission.

SERVICE 25. SELF IN TRAINING
1. Ps. 92:1-2, 4-5.
2. Acts 10:34-35; I Thess. 4:9; Gal. 3:26; I John 4:16, 19, 21.
3. Copyright 1948 by Guideposts Associates, Inc. Guideposts is an inspirational monthly magazine for all faiths published at Carmel, New York. $2.00 per year.
4. Jas. 1:26-27.
5. "Come Forth, O Christian Youth." From *Two More New Hymns for Youth by Youth,* copyright 1956 by The Hymn Society of America, used by permission.

SERVICE 26. THANKS BE TO GOD
1. I Chr. 16:8-9. From the Revised Standard Version of the Bible, Copyrighted 1946 and 1952.
2. Ps. 100; 105:1-4.
3. Used by permission.

SERVICE 27. ALL ARE BROTHERS
1. John 4:23-24.
2. Mark 12:29-31; Gal. 3:28; Isa. 26:3; 54:13; 32:18; John 14:27; Isa. 11:9.
3. From *Stories for Growing* by Alice Geer Kelsey. Used by permission of Abingdon Press.
4. Adapted. Used by permission.

SERVICE 28. WHO WILL BE FREE?
1. Lev. 25:10; II Cor. 3:17; Matt. 7:12.
2. By Alice Geer Kelsey. From *Stories for Growing.* Used by permission of Abingdon Press.
3. Used by permission.

SERVICE 29. PUTTING FIRST THINGS FIRST
1. Ps. 121:1-2.
2. Pss. 119:10; 86:11; 119:26-27; 19:14.
3. By Margaret Eggleston. From *Fireside Stories for Girls in Their Teens.* Used by permission of Harper & Bros.
4. Matt. 4:18-20.
5. Used by permission of the Hymn Society of America.

SERVICE 30. HE IS RISEN
1. Isa. 53:4-5.
2. Matt. 28:1-8.
3. By Roy L. Smith. From Salvation Army *War Cry.* Used by permission.

SERVICE 31. CHRIST LIVES TODAY
1. Rom. 14:9; Isa. 42:10.
2. Matt. 27:54, 62-66; 28:11-13, 15.
3. By G. L. Wind. From *This Day* Magazine, April, 1955. Used by permission.

SERVICE 32. WISE MEN BRING THEIR GIFTS
1. Isa. 9:6; Matt. 2:1-2, 7-11.
2. By Fred J. Jordan. Used by permission.
3. By Mack B. Stokes. Used by permission.

NOTES

SERVICE 33. CHRISTMAS FOR EVERYONE
1. John 1:1, 14; Gal. 4:4; John 3:16-17.
2. By Fred J. Jordan. Used by permission.
3. Used by permission.

SERVICE 34. WHEN TRIALS COME
1. Isa. 53:3, 6, 7; Luke 23:13-14, 20-21, 26.
2. By Chester A. McPheeters. From *Together,* May, 1957. Used by permission.

SERVICE 35. SON OF STEPHEN
1. Used by permission.

SOURCES FOR HYMNS

Code: The letter refers to the hymnal, and the number to the page on which the hymn is found in the hymnal.

A Charge to Keep I Have
  B—157; C—376; E—379; G—186;
  H—289; I—196; J—161; M—287;
  N—500; R—240; T—203; W—373;
  X—358

A Glory Gilds the Sacred Page
  C—170; M—388; R—107; T—74;
  X—186

All Glory, Laud, and Honor
  C—86; D—113; F—90; M—128;
  N—11; P—146; T—142; W—221;
  X—151; Y—74

All Hail the Power of Jesus' Name
  A—135; B—1; C—131; D—135;
  E—362; F—122; G—54; H—116;
  I—198; J—114; M—164; N—142;
  P—192; R—8; T—133; W—252;
  X—132; Y—426

A Mighty Fortress Is Our God
  A—210; B—38; C—195; D—51;
  E—351; F—38; G—6; H—308; I—
  168; J—41; M—67; N—259; P—

266; R—43; S—6; T—37; W—155;
  X—40; Y—150

Angels, from the Realms of Glory
  B—145; C—27; D—86; F—69;
  H—49; I—283; J—71; M—87; N—
  80; P—124; T—91; W—192; X—
  76; Y—31

"Are Ye Able?"
  B—396; E—174; G—184; J—189;
  M—268; W—360; X—351

At Length There Dawns the Glorious Day
  E—256; F—288; H—335; J—251;
  M—469; N—390; W—511

Awake, Awake to Love and Work
  M—455; W—323

Be Thou My Vision
  A—236; F—115; J—174; P—325;
  W—321; X—62

Beneath the Cross of Jesus
  A—120; B—234; D—186; E—105;
  F—173; G—39; H—95; I—176;

228

J—91; M—144; N—125; P—162;
R—242; S—351; T—110; W—235;
X—345; Y—482

Break Thou the Bread of Life
A—71; B—192; D—157; E—101;
F—133; G—235; H—381; I—243;
J—132; M—387; N—412; P—216;
R—199; S—354; T—81; W—461;
X—178; Y—491

Breathe on Me, Breath of God
A—61; B—417; D—152; E—98;
F—130; G—76; J—123; M—180;
N—201; P—213; T—146; X—167;
Y—470

Christ for the World We Sing
B—267; C—218; D—319; E—355;
F—250; H—404; J—266; M—481;
N—369; P—378; R—20; T—262;
W—538; X—458; Y—311

Christ the Lord Is Risen Today
A—129; B—33; C—111; D—126;
E—331; F—104; G—48; H—118;
I—212; J—102; M—154; N—130;
P—165; R—94; T—120; W—239;
X—115; Y—107

Christ, Whose Glory Fills the Skies
C—450; H—455; J—20; M—32;
N—43; P—26; X—22; Y—208

Come, Ye Faithful, Raise the Strain
C—108; F—108; J—101; M—151;
N—134; P—168; S—363; W—242;
X—109; Y—106

Come, Ye Thankful People, Come
A—322; B—136; C—484; D—360;
F—18; G—27; H—483; I—141; J—
287; M—545; N—454; P—460; S—
364; T—307; W—593; X—490; Y
—363

Crown Him with Many Crowns
B—18; C—134; D—134; E—333;
F—120; G—66; H—115; I—114;
M—170; P—190; R—17; T—141;
W—250; X—152; Y—431

Dare to Be Brave
B—320; D—202; F—223; G—188;
I—266; R—166; T—401; X—411

Dear Lord and Father of Mankind
A—152; B—401; D—236; E—80;
F—150; G—137; H—242; I—238;
J—202; M—342; N—224; P—302;
R—280; S—366; T—63; W—411;
X—335; Y—467

Dear Master, in Whose Life I See
M—376; N—265; P—507; W—318

Draw Thou My Soul, O Christ
A—149; D—234; E—370; F—164;
G—151; H—250; J—160; M—297;
N—232; W—299; X—314

Fairest Lord Jesus
A—137; B—211; D—136; E—58;
F—119; G—55; H—72; J—113;
M—111; N—465; P—194; R—48;
S—369; T—102; W—261; X—159

Faith of Our Fathers! Living Still
B—201; D—203; E—109; F—224;
G—104; H—210; I—258; J—200;
M—256; N—220; P—267; R—211;
S—104; T—249; W—348; X—252;
Y—516

Fight the Good Fight
A—207; B—270; D—212; E—158;
F—228; G—204; H—299; J—201;
M—286; N—255; P—270; R—261;
S—375; T—200; W—376; X—406;
Y—557

For the Beauty of the Earth
A—46; B—246; C—292; D—55;
E—357; F—42; G—16; H—16; I—
264; J—59; M—18; N—168; P—71;
R—50; S—16; T—309; W—167;
X—153; Y—444

Forward Through the Ages
B—419; D—350; E—113; H—374;
N—400; W—498; X—463

Give of Your Best to the Master
B—366; F—176; G—189; I—32;
R—79; T—375; X—353

God of Grace and God of Glory
F—236; **G**—115; **M**—279; **W**—378;
X—465

God of Our Fathers, Whose Almighty
Hand
B—240; **C**—493; **D**—302; **E**—283;
F—271; **G**—226; **H**—342; **J**—272;
M—496; **N**—356; **P**—414; **T**—26;
W—551; **X**—54; **Y**—521

God of Our Youth, to Whom We Yield
A—162; **F**—179; **W**—608

God of the Strong, God of the Weak
E—217; **M**—457; **W**—311

God Save America
B—387; **D**—305; **F**—273; **N**—360;
W—547

God, Who Touchest Earth with Beauty
A—223; **D**—222; **F**—178; **G**—152;
J—304; **W**—315; **X**—45

Great Master, Touch Us
A—222; **F**—186; **W**—317

Happy the Home When God Is There
G—242; **M**—428; **X**—374

Hark! the Herald Angels Sing
A—77; **B**—142; **C**—25; **D**—80;
E—361; **F**—68; **G**—28; **H**—59;
I—284; **J**—66; **M**—86; **N**—91; **P**—
117; **R**—55; **S**—391; **T**—83; **W**—
189; **X**—81; **Y**—25

Hark, the Voice of Jesus Calling
B—407; **D**—162; **G**—185; **H**—283;
M—288; **N**—504; **S**—392; **T**—268;
X—440; **Y**—59

He Leadeth Me
B—422; **D**—71; **F**—54; **H**—46; **I**—
250; **J**—53; **M**—242; **N**—501; **P**—
106; **R**—206; **T**—59; **W**—405; **X**—
58; **Y**—478

Heralds of Christ
A—258; **F**—235; **G**—181; **H**—407;
J—264; **M**—482; **N**—375; **P**—379;
T—407; **W**—533; **X**—452; **Y**—320

Holy Spirit, Truth Divine
A—60; **D**—146; **E**—100; **F**—128;
I—319; **M**—173; **N**—496; **P**—208;
W—274

How Beauteous Were the Marks Divine
B—298; **M**—116; **T**—101

I Bind My Heart This Tide
A—121; **E**—143; **F**—205; **H**—243;
J—169; **P**—243; **S**—202; **W**—302

In Christ There Is No East or West
A—299; **D**—314; **E**—273; **F**—243;
G—221; **H**—375; **J**—234; **M**—507;
N—389; **P**—341; **R**—140; **W**—480;
X—443; **Y**—342

In the Cross of Christ I Glory
A—124; **B**—180; **C**—62; **D**—117;
E—377; **F**—95; **G**—43; **H**—375;
I—210; **J**—94; **M**—149; **N**—127;
P—154; **R**—86; **T**—113; **W**—237;
X—100; **Y**—64

Into the Woods My Master Went
A—119; **B**—420; **D**—121; **E**—84;
F—100; **H**—99; **I**—63; **M**—132;
N—126; **T**—114; **W**—225; **X**—90

It Came Upon the Midnight Clear
A—78; **B**—141; **C**—29; **D**—76;
E—245; **F**—64; **H**—58; **J**—73;
M—92; **N**—73; **P**—127; **R**—56;
S—416; **T**—85; **W**—191; **X**—71; **Y**
—23

I Would Be True
A—177; **B**—368; **D**—225; **E**—180;
F—180; **G**—119; **I**—23; **J**—309;
N—469; **R**—134; **S**—119; **W**—361

Jesus Shall Reign
A—305; **B**—150; **C**—219; **D**—310;
E—380; **F**—248; **G**—220; **H**—392;
I—188; **J**—267; **M**—479; **N**—373;

P—377; R—256; S—425; T—260;
W—527; X—116; Y—307

Jesus, Thou Joy of Loving Hearts
  C—354; F—147; G—57; H—67;
  J—206; M—345; N—415; P—354;
  S—427; T—134; W—419; X—136;
  Y—483

Joyful, Joyful, We Adore Thee
  A—43; D—48; E—49; F—6; G—3;
  H—25; I—3; J—5; M—12; P—5;
  R—53; T—52; W—95; X—44; Y
  —438

Just as I Am, Thine Own to Be
  A—145; B—411; D—181; E—136;
  F—171; G—143; H—280; J—310;
  N—428; R—68; S—131; W—297;
  X—249

Lamp of Our Feet
  A—72; D—160; H—139; J—133;
  W—436

Lead on, O King Eternal
  A—199; B—236; D—208; E—177;
  F—226; G—210; H—301; I—84;
  J—191; M—278; N—251; P—371;
  R—139; S—210; T—210; W—363;
  Y—550

Lord, Speak to Me, That I May Speak
  A—251; C—212; D—293; E—216;
  F—196; G—175; H—279; I—222;
  J—248; M—460; N—339; P—399;
  S—438; T—211; W—470; X—340;
  Y—538

Love Divine, All Loves Excelling
  A—67; B—19; C—276; D—231;
  E—356; F—153; G—111; H—21;
  I—2; J—176; M—372; N—270;
  P—308; R—81; S—440; T—183;
  W—379; X—2; Y—397

March on, O Soul, with Strength
  A—184; D—220; E—110; F—234;
  G—192; H—300; M—264; N—247;
  P—273; W—359; X—422

'Mid All the Traffic of the Ways
  A—159; F—165; G—165; H—237;
  J—204; M—341; P—322

More Love to Thee, O Christ
  B—218; D—200; F—191; G—110;
  H—224; I—240; J—168; M—364;
  N—146; P—315; R—283; S—148;
  T—195; W—390; X—292; Y—392

My Faith Looks Up to Thee
  A—155; B—209; C—360; D—190;
  F—211; G—103; H—194; I—236;
  J—211; M—213; N—498; P—285;
  R—270; S—445; T—168; W—355;
  X—257; Y—375

My God, I Thank Thee
  A—51; D—361; E—204; F—11;
  H—73; J—183; M—9; N—11; P—
  73; T—49; W—109; Y—447

My Master Was a Worker
  D—285; G—183; W—500

Now in the Days of Youth
  A—146; D—175; F—169; G—207;
  J—308; N—477; W—300

Now, on Land and Sea Descending
  G—23; H—462; J—27; M—45;
  N—57; P—47; S—23; T—462; W
  —141; X—28

Now Thank We All Our God
  A—325; C—283; D—358; E—303;
  F—17; J—289; M—7; N—12; P—
  459; R—292; S—560; T—44; W—
  598; X—491; Y—443

O Brother Man, Fold to Thy Heart
  A—244; B—403; D—283; E—258;
  F—260; J—254; M—466; P—403;
  T—275; W—515; X—447; Y—539

O Come, All Ye Faithful
  A—83; B—143; D—89; E—298;
  F—74; G—30; H—56; J—69;
  M—96; N—105; P—116; S—452;
  T—90; W—205; X—66; Y—42

O for a Heart to Praise My God
  C—264; G—176; H—257; J—177;
  M—370; P—260; S—456; Y—389

O for a Thousand Tongues to Sing
B—5; C—135; G—67; H—68; I—
229; J—112; M—162; P—199; R—
71; S—457; T—128; W—262; X—
129; Y—428

O God, Beneath Thy Guiding Hand
A—270; D—357; E—116; F—275;
H—462; I—93; J—290; M—493;
N—347; P—462; W—543

O God, Our Help in Ages Past
B—435; C—505; E—30; G—145;
H—77; M—533; N—177; P—77;
R—49; S—145; T—39; W—585;
X—286; Y—168

O Jesus, I Have Promised
A—196; B—187; D—187; E—369;
F—174; H—253; I—189; J—165;
M—226; N—196; P—268; R—239;
S—462; T—193; W—308; X—386;
Y—515

O Jesus, Thou Art Standing
A—148; B—242; C—322; D—174;
E—375; F—201; H—170; I—247;
J—139; M—197; N—246; P—228;
T—179; W—279; X—346; Y—386

O Little Town of Bethlehem
A—82; B—144; C—31; D—78;
E—330; F—66; G—31; H—65;
I—281; J—64; M—100; N—74;
P—121; R—57; S—464; T—82;
W—184; X—75; Y—27

O Love Divine and Golden
G—170; I—65; M—430; N—292;
P—485; R—129

O Master, Let Me Walk with Thee
A—197; B—202; D—182; E—214;
F—166; G—116; H—271; I—263;
J—245; M—259; N—291; P—364;
R—19; S—468; T—274; W—306;
X—426; Y—537

O Master Workman of the Race
A—98; D—106; E—74; F—85;
G—59; H—82; J—86; M—118;

N—328; P—140; R—62; W—210;
X—441

Once to Every Man and Nation
A—220; D—184; E—240; F—221;
H—373; J—249; M—263; N—326;
P—373; W—558; X—418; Y—547

Open My Eyes
B—351; D—192; F—189; I—34;
J—227; R—251; X—312

O Perfect Love
C—415; H—484; J—296; M—431;
N—430; P—484; X—501; Y—300

O Son of Man, Our Hero
A—109; E—79; F—114; P—177;
W—220

O Son of Man, Thou Madest Known
A—188; D—207; E—175; F—197;
G—61; M—121; N—329; S—61;
Y—217

O Young and Fearless Prophet
G—212; M—266; W—362

O Zion, Haste
A—306; B—151; C—224; D—308;
E—270; F—240; G—222; H—395;
I—217; J—257; M—475; N—372;
P—382; R—131; S—474; T—264;
W—529; X—451; Y—314

Rejoice, Ye Pure in Heart
A—27; B—285; D—139; E—199;
F—124; G—9; J—209; M—358;
N—476; P—297; R—181; S—483;
T—47; W—418; X—17; Y—555

Rise Up, O Men of God
A—254; B—186; D—288; E—224;
F—258; G—203; H—274; J—252;
M—267; N—313; P—401; W—374;
X—445; Y—541

Silent Night, Holy Night
A—81; B—146; C—530; D—83;
E—302; F—73; G—33; H—60;
I—285; J—74; M—106; N—98;

P—132; R—59; S—494; W—188;
X—72; Y—16

Sing with All the Sons of Glory
G—49; M—150

Spirit of God, Descend upon My Heart
A—62; D—148; E—99; F—127;
G—75; H—125; J—125; M—179;
N—233; P—204; R—137; T—150;
W—272; X—166; Y—129

Take My Life, and Let It Be
A—198; B—174; C—382; D—221;
E—142; F—175; G—131; H—272;
I—83; J—166; M—225; N—195;
P—242; R—244; S—501; T—327;
W—296; X—357; Y—510

Take Thou Our Minds
D—11; F—168; G—276; J—311;
P—245

Teach Us, O Lord, True Brotherhood
D—281; F—256; H—370; N—304

The Body, Lord, Is Ours to Keep
A—164; F—187; G—134

The Day of Resurrection
A—127; C—115; D—128; E—301;
F—102; H—106; J—99; M—159;
N—132; P—166; R—98; W—247;
X—111; Y—105

The First Noel
A—79; B—140; D—82; E—328;
F—70; G—35; J—72; M—97;
N—97; P—129; S—231; W—197;
X—63; Y—40

The Hidden Years at Nazareth
A—97; D—101; E—73; F—83

The Light of God Is Falling
D—279; F—254; G—213; H—376;
J—250; M—468; N—309; P—400;
W—486; X—442

The Morning Light Is Breaking
B—12; C—230; D—307; F—239;

H—406; J—260; M—487; N—364;
P—389; R—132; T—271; W—524;
X—448; Y—313

There's a Song in the Air
A—84; F—79; G—34; M—98;
N—82; W—198; X—69

The Voice of God Is Calling
D—284; E—235; F—202; G—205;
M—454; N—337; W—490

The Whole, Wide World for Jesus
D—313; F—242; T—270

This Is My Father's World
A—39; D—52; E—51; F—43;
G—11; H—332; I—10; J—60;
M—72; N—464; P—70; R—31;
S—11; T—406; W—171; X—59;
Y—487

Thou Art the Way
C—368; D—271; F—214; H—81;
J—167; M—332; P—254; S—516;
T—172; Y—390

Thy Kingdom Come, O Lord
D—326; F—280; G—257; N—388;
P—425; W—562

'Tis Midnight; and on Olive's Brow
B—295; F—98; H—96; I—143;
J—92; M—133; N—119; P—119;
R—152; T—105; W—232; X—104

Truehearted, Wholehearted, Faithful
and Loyal
F—177; I—28; M—255; R—226;
S—278; T—383; X—410

We Gather Together
E—29; G—12; J—10; M—20; N—
29; W—117; X—492

We Plow the Fields and Scatter
A—323; C—486; D—356; E—46;
F—55; J—288; M—544; N—473;
P—464; W—594; X—493; Y—364

We Thank Thee, Lord, Thy Paths of Service Lead
A—249; B—301; D—287; E—223; F—203; G—206; M—458; N—340; P—367; W—495

We've a Story to Tell to the Nations
A—302; B—379; D—306; F—238; G—215; I—146; J—261; M—501; N—374; R—124; T—261; W—530; X—455

When I Survey the Wondrous Cross
A—123; B—191; C—97; D—118; E—376; F—96; G—44; H—88; I—215; J—97; M—148; N—122; P—152; R—247; S—532; T—108; W—228; X—99; Y—503

When Morning Gilds the Skies
A—2; B—7; C—310; D—1; E—201; F—19; G—20; H—453; I—1; J—21; M—31; N—41; P—3; R—26; S—533; T—2; W—135; X—23; Y—416

Where Cross the Crowded Ways of Life
A—265; B—405; C—235; D—268; E—60; F—253; G—214; H—330; I—230; J—268; M—465; N—140; P—410; R—24; S—536; T—276; W—519; X—464; Y—351

Work, for the Night Is Coming
B—243; I—235; M—293; N—502; S—538; T—272; X—424

SELECTED BIBLIOGRAPHY

WORSHIP FOR JUNIOR HIGHS

Applegarth Margaret T. *Restoring Worship*. New York: Harper & Bros., 1949.
Bowie, Walter Russell. *The Bible Story for Boys and Girls—New Testament*. Nashville: Abingdon Press, 1951.
——. *The Bible Story for Boys and Girls—Old Testament*. Nashville: Abingdon Press, 1952.
——. *Christ Be With Me*. Nashville: Abingdon Press, 1958.
——. *The Story of the Bible*. Nashville: Abingdon Press, 1934.
——. *The Story of Jesus for Young People*. New York: Charles Scribner's Sons, 1937.
Bowman, Clarice. *Restoring Worship*. Nashville: Abingdon Press, 1951.
Edgar, Mary S. *Under Open Skies*. Toronto, Can.: Clarke, Irwin & Co.
Gilbert, Clark R. *Devotions for Youth*. New York: Association Press, 1943.
Jones, E. Stanley. *How to Pray*. Nashville: Abingdon Press, 1951.
Myers, A. J. William, ed. *Enriching Worship*. New York: Harper & Bros., 1949.
Paulsen, Irwin G. *The Church School and Worship*. Nashville: Abingdon Press, 1940.
Pease, Dorothy Wells. *Meditations Under the Sky*. Nashville: Abingdon Press, 1957.
Porter, David R., ed. *Worship Resources for Youth*. New York: Association Press, 1948.
Schmitz, Charles H. *Windows Toward God*. Nashville: Abingdon Press, 1950.
Smith, Roy L. *Making a Go of Life*. Nashville: Abingdon Press, 1948.
——. *New Light from Old Lamps*. Nashville: Abingdon Press, 1953.
Stafford, Thomas A. *Christian Symbolism in the Evangelical Churches*. Nashville: Abingdon Press, 1942.
Watson, Lillian Eichler, ed. *Light from Many Lamps*. New York: Simon & Schuster, 1951.
Redhead John, A. *Getting to Know God*. Nashville: Abingdon Press, 1954.

POEMS

Armstrong, O. V. and Helen, comps. *Prayer Poems*. Nashville: Abingdon Press, 1942.
Bever, Patricia. *Steppingstones of the Spirit*. New York: Association Press, 1951.
Clark, Thomas Curtis, comp. *The Golden Book of Religious Verse*. New York: Garden City Publishing Co., 1941.
——. *Poems of Justice*. Chicago: Willet, Clark & Co., 1929.
—— and Hazel, eds. *Christ in Poetry*. New York: Association Press, 1952.
—— and Robert Earle, comps. *Poems for the Great Days*. Nashville: Abingdon Press, 1948.
—— and Gillespie, Esther A., comps. *1000 Quotable Poems*. Chicago: Willet, Clark & Co., 1937.
Cushman, Ralph S. *Hilltop Verses and Prayers*. Nashville: Abingdon Press, 1945.
——. *Practicing the Presence*. Nashville: Abingdon Press, 1936.

———— and Robert E. *More Hilltop Verses and Prayers.* Nashville: Abingdon Press, 1949.

Gibran, Kahlil. *The Prophet.* New York: Alfred A. Knopf, 1923.

Harkness, Georgia. *Be Still and Know.* Nashville: Abingdon Press, 1953.

Hill, Caroline, ed. *The World's Great Religious Poetry.* New York: The Macmillan Co., 1923.

Kagawa, Toyohiko. *Songs from the Slums.* Nashville: Abingdon Press, 1935.

Markham, Edwin. *Poems.* New York: Harper & Bros., 1950.

Morgan, Angela. *Selected Poems.* New York: Dodd, Mead & Co., 1926.

Morrison, James Dalton, ed. *Masterpieces of Religious Verse.* New York: Harper & Bros., 1948.

Mudge, James, comp. and ed. *Poems with Power to Strengthen the Soul.* Nashville: Abingdon Press, 1907.

Oxenham, John. *Gentlemen—The King!* Boston: Pilgrim Press, 1928.

————. *Hearts Courageous.* New York: Methodist Book Concern, 1918.

————. *Selected Poems.* New York: Harper & Bros., 1948.

Piety, Chauncey R. *General Sam Houston, and Other Poems.* Emory University, Ga.: Banner Press, 1943.

Van Dyke, Henry. *Collected Poems.* New York: Charles Scribner's Sons, 1920.

York, Esther Baldwin. *Scarf of Stars.* Orange, Calif.: John T. McInnis, 1953.

STORIES

Andrews, Roy Chapman. *Nature's Ways.* New York: Crown Publishers, 1951.

Bartlett, Robert M. *They Dare to Believe.* New York: Association Press, 1952.

————. *They Did Something About It.* New York: Association Press. 1939.

Bolton, Sarah. *Famous Men of Science.* New York: Thomas Y. Crowell Co., 1941.

————. *Lives of Girls Who Became Famous.* New York: Thomas Y. Crowell Co. 1925.

————. *Lives of Poor Boys Who Became Famous.* New York: Thomas Y. Crowell Co., 1947.

Cather, K. Dunlap. *Boyhood Stories of Famous Men.* New York: Century Co., 1916.

————. *Girlhood Stories of Famous Women.* New York: Century Co., 1924.

Cheley, Frank H. *Stories for Talks to Boys.* New York: Association Press, 1932.

Eddy, Sherwood. *Pathfinders of the World Missionary Crusade.* Nashville: Abingdon Press, 1945.

Eggleston Margaret. *Fireside Stories for Girls in Their Teens.* New York: George H. Doran Co., 1921.

Hazeltine, Alice I, comp. *Children's Stories to Read or Tell.* Nashville: Abingdon Press, 1949.

————. *We Grew Up in America.* Nashville: Abingdon Press, 1954.

Hodges, Graham. *Fifty Children's Sermons.* Nashville: Abingdon Press, 1957.

Hume, Edward H. *Doctors Courageous.* New York: Harper & Bros., 1950.

Kelsey, Alice Geer. *Stories for Growing.* Nashville: Abingdon Press, 1955.

Lantz, J. Edward, ed. *Best Religious Stories.* New York: Association Press. 1948.

————. *Stories of Christian Living.* New York: Association Press. 1950.

Malone, Ted. *Favorite Stories.* New York: Doubleday & Co., 1950.

Mathews, Basil. *Book of Missionary Heroes.* New York: Harper & Bros., 1922.

McNeer, May Y., and Ward, Lynd K. *Armed with Courage.* Nashville: Abingdon Press. 1957.

——. *John Wesley*. Nashville: Abingdon Press, 1951.

——. *Martin Luther*. Nashville: Abingdon Press, 1953.

Parkman, Mary R. *Heroines of Service*. New York: Century Co., 1917.

Peale, Norman Vincent, ed. *Faith Made Them Champions*. Carmel, N.Y.: Guideposts Associates, 1954.

Broomell, Anna Pettit, ed. *The Children's Story Caravan*. New York: J. B. Lippincott Co., 1935.

Sawyers, Mott R. *Famous Friends of God*. New York: Fleming H. Revell Co., 1933.

Sheean, Vincent. *Thomas Jefferson: Father of Democracy*. New York: Random House, 1953.

Stewart, Mary. *The Shepherd of Us All*. New York: Fleming H. Revell Co., 1913.

Stidger, William L. *The Human Side of Greatness*. New York: Harper & Bros., 1940.

——. *More Sermons in Stories*. Nashville: Abingdon-Cokesbury Press, 1944.

——. *There Are Sermons in Stories*. Nashville: Abingdon Press, 1942.

Turnbull, Agnes S. *Far Above Rubies*. New York: Fleming H. Revell Co., 1926.

Wallace, Archer. *The Field of Honor*. Nashville: Abingdon Press, 1949.

——. *100 Stories for Boys*. Nashville: Abingdon Press, 1947.

——. *Overcoming Handicaps*. New York: George H. Doran Co., 1927.

——. *In Spite of All*. Nashville: Abingdon Press, 1945.

——. *Stories of Grit*. New York: Harper & Bros., 1930.

PRAYER

Abernethy, Jean Beaven, ed. *Meditations for Women*. Nashville: Abingdon Press, 1947.

Bowie, Walter Russell. *Christ Be with Me*. Nashville: Abingdon Press, 1958.

——. *Lift Up Your Hearts*. Nashville: Abingdon Press, 1956.

Buttrick, George A. *Prayer*. Nashville: Abingdon Press, 1942.

Campbell, Donald J. *The Adventure of Prayer*. Nashville: Abingdon Press, 1949.

Clough, William A. *Father, We Thank Thee*. Nashville: Abingdon Press, 1949.

Cushman, Ralph S. *Hilltop Verses and Prayers*. Nashville: Abingdon Press, 1945.

—— and Robert E. *More Hilltop Verses and Prayers*. Nashville: Abingdon Press, 1949.

Edmonds, Henry M. *Beginning the Day*. Nashville: Abingdon Press, 1952.

Ewing, Harold and Dorothy, comps. *Youth at Prayer*. Nashville: The Upper Room, 1957.

Finegan, Jack. *Book of Student Prayers*. New York: Association Press, 1946.

Harkness, Georgia. *Be Still and Know*. Nashville: Abingdon Press, 1953.

——. *The Glory of God*. Nashville: Abingdon Press, 1943.

——. *Prayer and the Common Life*. Nashville: Abingdon Press, 1948.

——. *Through Christ Our Lord*. Nashville: Abingdon Press, 1950.

Harlow, Samuel Ralph. *Prayers for Times Like These*. New York: Association Press, 1942.

Hayward, Percy R. *Young People's Prayers*. New York: Association Press, 1945.

Hoyland, J. S. *A Book of Prayers for Youth*. New York: Association Press, 1939.

Morton, Richard K. *A Book of Prayers for Young People*. Nashville: Abingdon Press, 1935.

Murrell, Gladys C. *Channels of Devotion*. Nashville: Abingdon Press, 1948.

——. *Glimpses of Grace.* Nashville: Abingdon Press, 1941.

——. *Patterns for Devotion.* Nashville: Abingdon Press, 1950.

Newman, John H., tr. *The Private Devotions of Lancelot Andrewes.* Nashville: Abingdon Press, 1950.

Pease, Dorothy Wells. *Meditations Under the Sky.* Nashville: Abingdon Press, 1957.

Wyon, Olive. *Consider Him.* Nashville: Abingdon Press, 1957.

INDEX OF STORIES AND SUBJECTS